ISBN 978 1 905184 87 3

L M S JOURNAL

NUMBER THIRTY-THREE

Contents

The locomotives of some of the LMS constituent companies were longlived and one type that remained in service well into the BR period was the ex-Caledonian 0–6–0. In this picture, taken at Motherwell on 2nd August 1938, we see No. 17301 which was built at St. Rollox in 1887 and withdrawn from service in 1948 without carrying its allocated British Railways number. However, No. 17300 was not withdrawn until 1962 and No. 17302 until 1963, which rather makes the point about their longevity.

L. HANSON

EDITORIAL

With one of the worst winters now over, it is pleasing to write this editorial during a sunny April day and to be able to look forward to Summer, a most enjoyable time when I can read manuscripts and look at photographs while sitting in the garden! In this issue we have a mixture of articles that should appeal to readers who are interested in the LMS during the years when it was an independent company and after 1948 when it was part of the nationalized British Railways system. Rather like the articles in our sister journal *Midland Record*, I believe the story of our railway system can only be told if you look at it 'from inception, through grouping into nationalization', and I hope this is how we present the story of the LMS.

I am always pleased to feature something different, and under this heading we have Neil Burgess's contribution on how the Somerset & Dorset Joint Railway handled some aspects of road cartage, whilst from Keith Miles we have a railwayman's story of lodging turns and what it was like. Prior to the Second World War, lodging was commonplace, but after 1939 the number of lodging turns were reduced.

I recall being told by a driver that it was because of the problems of rationing; whether this is true I cannot say, but in my experience during the 1950s, many turns that pre-1939 could have been lodging turns, were now worked by one set of men from A to B and another set from B to C, and so on, rather than one set which could have gone from A to D. Another pleasing article by Keith Miles is about the old North Staffordshire Railway, my favourite small constituent company, and a further article about this line will appear in the next issue. Finally, a somewhat different article is by John Jennison, which examines the LMS Company's policy when purchasing locomotives from 'The Trade', as the private companies that built locomotives were known. I believe it is articles like this that makes our approach to recording railway history rather different from most, and is based upon the experience gained when editing the formative editions of *Midland Record* where I found that lesser known subjects attracted a lot of favourable reader comment.

Bob Essery
bobessery@gowhite.com
www.lmsjournal.com

Designed by Paul Karau. Printed by Amadeus Press, Cleckheaton.
Published by WILD SWAN PUBLICATIONS LTD.
1-3 Hagbourne Road, Didcot, Oxon, OX11 8DP. Tel: 01235 816478

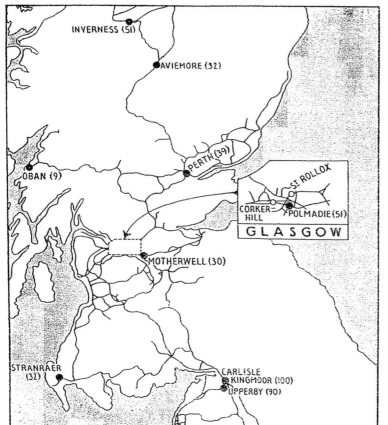

L.M.S.R. LOCOMOTIVE DEPOTS WHERE TRAINMEN'S HOSTELS ARE PROVIDED

Hostel					No. of beds
Aintree	...	...	...	...	86
Aston	...	...	...	...	42
Aviemore	...	...	...	...	32
Blackpool	...	...	...	...	56
Bletchley	...	...	...	...	8
Burton	...	...	...	...	32
Bushbury	...	...	...	...	18
Camden	...	...	...	...	90
Carlisle (Kingmoor)	...	...	...	...	100
Carlisle (Upperby)	...	...	...	...	90
Crewe	...	...	...	...	105
Cricklewood	...	...	...	...	31
Derby	...	...	...	...	42
Edge Hill	...	...	...	...	55
Farnley Junction	...	...	...	...	42
Gushetfaulds (Polmadie)	...	...	...	...	51
Holyhead	...	...	...	...	33
Inverness	...	...	...	...	51
Kentish Town	...	...	...	...	82
Leeds (Holbeck)	...	...	...	...	20
Leicester	...	...	...	...	14
Longsight	...	...	...	...	42
Motherwell	...	...	...	...	30
Mold Junction	...	...	...	...	40
Newton Heath	...	...	...	...	66
Northampton	...	...	...	...	19
Oban	...	...	...	...	9
Patricroft	...	...	...	...	61
Perth	...	...	...	...	39
Peterborough	...	...	...	...	34
Preston	...	...	...	...	40
Rugby	...	...	...	...	44
Saltley	...	...	...	...	92
Sheffield	...	...	...	...	17
Shrewsbury	...	...	...	...	40
Springs Branch	...	...	...	...	40
Stafford	...	...	...	...	32
Stranraer	...	...	...	...	32
Swansea	...	...	...	...	15
Toton	...	...	...	...	73
Wakefield	...	...	...	...	72
Wellingborough	...	...	...	...	56
Willesden	...	...	...	...	79

Total hostels, 43   2,052

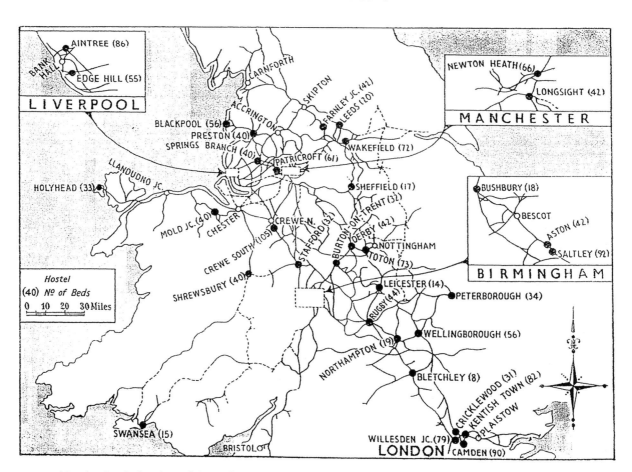

Map showing the locations of the LMS lodging houses in 1947. Reproduced by permission of The Railway Magazine.

Of Booking-off Turns and Barracks

by KEITH MILES

A 1951 view of the unique coaling plant at Edge Hill, where the loaded coal wagons were propelled up a ramp to unload into the top of the three 40-ton bunkers. On the left, an unrebuilt 'Scot' was going up to Engine Shed Junction which, with the adjacent lodging house, is just out of sight around the corner.
W. POTTER/
KEITH MILES COLLECTION

On this subject, a photograph caption in *LMS Reflections* (Bob Essery & Nigel Harris, Silver Link Publishing, 1986) probably says it all: 'Before World War II lodging turns were common place and frequently disliked by many engine crews. In those days official barracks were frequently located in less than desirable locations – adjacent to noisy shunting yards for example – whilst at other locations where men lodged there was no alternative but to take private lodgings. These varied in quality and it was not unknown for both men to have to sleep in the same bed. It was a hard life which would not be accepted today.'

This was a sentiment echoed by Ken Stokes of Grimesthorpe: "Not many men in middle life relished the idea of frequent trips which entailed lodging away from home, mainly at railway barracks. Some of these were situated in anything but salubrious surroundings: Edge Hill at Liverpool, Upperby at Carlisle, Holbeck at Leeds, to instance three of them, were all within fifty yards of a coal stage and that was not conducive to sound slumber!" I can vouch for that since I once spent a night at Edge Hill barracks when I was at Willesden on a double trip from Camden with driver Ernie Price on the 11.50 Euston – Liver-

pool, Lime Street, returning the next day with the 8.15 Lime Street – Euston. In 1914 Edge Hill had been provided with what turned out to be unique in this country, a 'Hennibrique System' coaling plant where the wagons were propelled up a ramp to discharge directly into the tops of the three 40-ton bunkers. Not only was I disturbed by the crashes and bangs of these proceedings but just outside my 'bedroom' window was Engine Shed Junction and every loco going down onto the shed whistled to let the bobby in No.11 box know it had cleared the points!

Since the barracks, hostels or lodging houses (all three titles appeared in common parlance) were originally intended for locomen, it was inevitable that they were located adjacent to the sheds. I have in my possession a copy of a letter (reproduced herewith) issued from C.R. Byrom's offices in 1933 listing the then 'Company's Barracks' in England and Wales. This makes an interesting comparison with the other accompanying list and map which appeared in 'LMSR Hostels for Trainmen', *Railway Magazine*, March/April 1947. The article claimed, incidentally, that, 'the first of these hostels was opened at Kentish Town by the Midland Railway fifty years ago', that is in 1897. Nonetheless, an etching of the

Wellingborough lodging house appeared in William's *The Midland Railway*, published in 1876.

Comparing the two lists, five of the 1933 barracks had disappeared by 1947: Abergavenny, Carlisle (Midland), Copley Hill (Leeds), Crewe North and Stockport. I don't know anything about the first three but Crewe North was located in Mill Street on the south side of the Chester line overbridge. Built in 1867, containing 42 beds, it ceased to function coincident with the rear extension of the Crewe South barrack in Gresty Road early in World War II. Thereafter, for a time, it became a Ministry of Labour hostel and, as such, featured in the demise of a possible budding railway career. A young friend and former fellow Kings Langley linesider had decided to follow me onto the railway as an LMS Engineering Apprentice (despite his father being an LNER clerk at King's Cross). He secured a place at Crewe, was found lodgings in the hostel and put to work on the Erecting Shop stripping pits. I regret that the filth of the latter and the discomfort of the former dimmed his ardour and he went back to college to train as a doctor.

Stockport barracks, according to Rowsley's Kye Gilbert, was, "two houses knocked into one just outside Edgeley shed,

E.R.O. 48030

LONDON MIDLAND AND SCOTTISH RAILWAY COMPANY

Chief Commercial and Chief Operating Managers' Depts.

DERBY.   SW.160.OW.   Cir. No. 47.33.

7th Nov. 1933.

LIST OF COMPANY'S LODGING HOUSES.

I enclose a list of stations and depots in England and Wales at which there are Company's Lodging Houses, and in each case where your staff book off to lodge at these depots the usual deduction of 1/- should be made.

There is also a number of depots in the Western Division where lodgings are provided by private lodging house keepers, the accounts for which are paid by the Company and not by the men, and I attach list of these also. These will, of course, be eliminated as and when the present lodging house keepers go out of business but meanwhile when booking off at the depots where such lodging houses are situated should be dealt with in the same way as men using the ordinary barracks.

Receipt of this Circular need NOT be acknowledged.

for C.R.B..ROW.

District Loco Supt.,
or
Running Shed Foreman.

Stations and depots at which there are Company's Barracks. (England and Wales)

Abergavenny
Aintree
Aston *

Blackpool
Bletchley *
Burton *
Bushbury

Camden
Carlisle N.
Carlisle W. **
Copley Hill
Crewe North
Crewe South
Cricklewood

Derby

Edge Hill *

Farnley Jc.

Holyhead

Kentish Town

Leeds **
Leicester *
Longsight

Mold Jc.

Newton Heath
Northampton

Patricroft
Preston *
Peterboro'

Rugby *

Saltley
Sheffield
Shrewsbury **
Springs Branch (Wigan)
Stafford *
Stockport
Swansea

Toton

Wakefield
Wellingboro *
Willesden

Of the Midland and Western Division barracks listed, those marked with an asterisk were, to my certain knowledge, located adjacent to the sheds, and those with double asterisks actually in the shed yard.

The former Crewe North hostel in 1973, just prior to demolition. The Crewe—Chester line is seen crossing Mill Street in the background.

A. C. BAKER

Crewe South hostel, Gresty Road, in 1950. The early 1940s extension at the rear can be clearly seen. Apart from using the facilities on several occasions from Willesden or Camden, I passed it every day from my digs in Claughton Avenue while working at the Divisional Motive Power Superintendent's offices in the platform 1 and 2 buildings at the station.   K. MILES

but I used to go into private lodgings. I used to go down into Cheadle Heath where we used to lodge on t'Hole in t'Wall job on t'Midland, with Mrs Clayton or Mrs Smith. It were a Rowsley – Ancoats, then light engine to Heaton Mersey and lodge. Then we'd be on at 6/25 at night, work to Trafford Park from Cheadle then the 9/55 Trafford Park – Rowsley, relief on arrival." On being asked why it was known as the Hole in t'Wall job, he said, "That were a pub at Stockport that a lot of railwaymen used to go in." In any event, I was spared having to lodge at Stockport when I worked the 9/50 FF2 Camden – Adswood with Ted Bloggs, a former Devons Road man who'd moved to Willesden for promotion. I discovered afterwards from George Bushell that he wasn't well liked. "He was used to working with Jinties and on main line trains he burnt more coal than was normal or necessary" – that struck a chord!

Anyway, we were relieved on arrival at Adswood, walked to Stockport and went as passenger to Longsight and booked off at 6.50. Now, I can't remember exactly where the barracks were but they were somewhere near the Belle Vue Pleasure Gardens' speedway stadium and my daytime slumbers were disrupted by the repeated roar of riders practising. As for the hostel itself, I don't think it had changed much since before the war, as described by Ken Stokes on the occasion of a summer Sunday excursion to Blackpool. The route was via the Dore and Chinley line to Manchester, Belle Vue where relief had been afforded at Engine Shed Junction by Belle Vue men who worked the train forward. Ken and his mate booked off then walked the 1½ miles to Longsight hostel. "The hostel was a typical LNW set-up, a cheerless place, even with a huge fire in the dining room. And what a dining room! Wooden tables, none too clean, and ironclad forms. The bedrooms were mere cubicles, with walls that did not reach the ceiling." However, rested or not, we booked on again at 8/35 that night to work the 9/20 FF2 Stockport – Willesden where we booked off at 4.10.

I never got as far as Carlisle but on a couple of occasions I worked the southern leg of 'The Doodlebug', the 2/55 FF1 Camden – Glasgow, lodging at Crewe after booking off at the South Shed at 6/45. We'd been relieved on arrival in Basford Hall yard by a Crewe South set who took the engine to the shed after any necessary detaching and attaching. Meantime, a

Crewe North set came with a fresh engine for the run to Carlisle, departing at 6/56. They were relieved by an Upperby set on arrival at Carlisle No.12 SB opposite the shed. While they went to the shed to book off, the Upperby men took the train to Kingmoor where a fresh engine and men awaited to take the train on to Glasgow, Buchanan Street, the Crewe engine being brought back light to Upperby. As for the Crewe men, Pete Johnson recalled his first trip in 1952–"Then came the trudge uphill to the railway hostel, or the lodge or barracks as they were sometimes called; the first time for me to sample this particular kind of hospitality. I was pleased to find that everything was very clean, and I was shown by Ben [his driver] where to put the various items of gear, cap, jacket and 'butty bag', to be left in the equipment room along with our overalls. Next we booked in and told the attendant who we were, what time we wanted to get up and the time of our return train. After giving us each a piece of soap and a towel, he allocated us to our bedrooms. I was quite surprised that we had one each, as I was under the impression that a set shared the same room. [That was the case at Kingmoor, I'm given to understand] I had heard old Western drivers say that not only did they sleep in the same room but that they sometimes even had to wait for someone to get up! But those were private lodgings, not barracks. Ben told me that, on the LM Region, at least, one always had a bedroom to oneself and that these were always well cared for, with fresh sheets on the bed. We had a much needed wash and then a three-course meal which, I recall, was all for the deduction of 1s.9d. from our booking-off allowance! As it was now about 2am we were both extremely tired and retired promptly to bed."

The hostel described by Pete was a new, modern building opened in the early 1940s on rising ground south of Upperby to replace the Nor'West establishment in the shed yard. Ken Stokes found it to be "excellent, clean, providing goods meals and with competent staff." However, it was a different story when temporary goods guard, Dick Fawcett, found himself at Carlisle at the end of a terrible journey in 1937. He'd suffered awful weather as well as having to stop several times en route to shunt out hot 'fat boxes'. "We ran into the goods loop at Durran Hill at 9/45 with just fifteen wagons left on the train. [He'd started with twenty-eight] I grabbed my traps, jumped out and was making my way to the station

to arrange a lift home when the sidings inspector called me back to speak to Control. They said, 'You've had a bad trip, but make your way to the barracks at Upperby Loco. We have booked a bed for you. Book off when you get there, then book on at 7.30 in the morning to work the Carlisle – Leeds semi-fitted.' I was in a right dismay; apparently this was the Leeds guard's back working and I argued that I was a single trip man, put on at Hellifield in an emergency. But I had to do as I was told – we had to in those days."

"I got some fish and chips in the barracks, then went to my room. This was a little cubicle with plywood partitions, perhaps six feet by seven, containing a single bed. The charge for a night's lodging was small and we got it refunded with the next week's wage. I did not sleep a wink; I could hear men from Crewe, Leicester, London, Birmingham, Scotland – locomen and guards from all over the country; some snoring, some just getting up for their return working, some coming in the worse for drink, quite a lot sitting and talking the night away, brewing up and smoking. Apart from this, I could hear engines going onto the shed. Some seemed to be whistling the night away; shunt engines all over the huge sidings complex at Carlisle acknowledging signals, popping here, popping there! Then, just outside was the coaling plant crashing and banging all night – lifting a ten-ton wagon of coal to a great height, turning it over and emptying it into a huge hopper, then doling it out in smaller loads into engine tenders."

Having mentioned Scotland, perhaps a word or two about the hostel in Glasgow, known variously as Polmadie, Gushetfaulds or Larkfield – the latter, so a former St.Rollox colleague tells me, because it was situated in the short Larkfield Street off Cathcart Road and overlooked the down WCML at Gushetfaulds. He also said that from the railway it appeared to be a WWII structure but he was unaware if it replaced or was added to an older building. Whatever the truth of the matter, it was not an inviting place if Kingmoor's Peter Brock's scathing description from 1958 is anything to go by. "The Larkfield hostel was the last place on earth that a weary railwayman could ever hope to get any rest, let alone a decent meal." As I've said, it was located off the Cathcart Road, noisy with a number of tram routes which, as it happens, a decade or so earlier, had seen my daily passage on a No.19, Mount Florida –

Springburn car from my 'digs' in Govanhill, across the city and up to St.Rollox. Being allocated a room on the other side of the building brought no respite since it was well within earshot of a busy scrapyard. Furthermore, it seems that on some evenings the noise of the crusher was replaced by the thump of a big bass drum as the local Salvation Army band undertook band practice in the hall across the road. Peter found that, "Taking refuge on the top floor was perhaps the best thing to do. With a good view of Langside Junction and a whistle codebook in your hand, the time could be passed trying to determine the routes of the passing trains by the shrieks and hoots from a conglomeration of sounds. No menu existed in this tartan bedlam. It was plain Hobson's choice; sausage and mash, stew, soup or porridge. Train crews from as far afield as Leeds and Crewe lodged here but by far the most numerous guests or 'victims' here were the Kingmoor goods link men. One day in 1957 they had virtually brought the Glasgow – Carlisle route to a standstill, by reason of a savage epidemic of dysentery caused, so it was rumoured, by their partaking of the foul Gorbals' stew."

Back to Willesden: in 1944, having moved into what had once been the Toton link, George Bushell found that it was by then mainly mineral traffic, relief at Rugby or Northampton to book off and work back the next day. "The hostel at North-ampton had been converted from some disused stables in the middle of the goods yard adjacent to what was Bridge Street station. The sleeping cubicles upstairs were just big enough for a single bed and a chair with the partitions in between in matchboarding. Always, day or night, the sound of heavy snoring echoed through these thin walls." Surprisingly, in view of the short distance, one week he and his mate were booked off at Bletchley every other trip, "and I found out it was true that the lodge was under the water tank." This singular building stood across the station yard from the Booking Office and originally held the offices and stores of the first engine shed, built at the same time, on the coming of the Buckinghamshire Railway's lines in the early 1850s. The shed, of less substantial construction, being only made of timber and galvanised iron, collapsed during a gale in 1872. The new shed was completed the following year with its own offices and the building took up its new role as a lodging house in 1877. The tank on its roof for loco supplies was fed by water pumped from a reservoir in the angle between the main and Oxford branch lines south of the station. When I knew the building, the tank had gone out of use and, by then, it was being used to accommodate Polish shed staff. Since they were all ex-soldiers, the term 'barracks' became particularly appropriate. There was also a band of them on each ashpit shift at Willesden, some being former high-ranking officers, but I'm uncertain as to whether they were similarly accommodated in the Willesden barracks.

By that time, 1949, the number of lodging turns at Willesden, in company with most other depots, was much reduced from the pre-war figure. As a result, only the crews on the 'fitteds', such as those described above, continued to their destinations, or mileage limit, and lodged. 140 miles was the distance equated to an eight-hour day with each subsequent 15 miles counting as an additional hour. The majority of northbound freights were relieved at Bletchley with the crews then reporting to Control from the relief cabin at the end of platform 8 to take up a return working. It was seldom their diagrammed job due to the congestion and delay on the up line being experienced at that time. I recall Rowsley's George Newton commenting, "In those days there were a lot of traffic with relief cabins everywhere. Cabins wi' a gang of men in waiting for trains." Take one occasion when I came back from Crewe on one of the aforementioned lodging turns; we signed on at the South Shed at 6.25 to relieve the 5.15 SO Maltese Cross from Liverpool at Salop Goods Junction. After a slow, faltering journey we were relieved at Northampton and made our way back to Willesden 'as passenger' where we signed off at 6/20, five minutes short of a twelve-hour day.

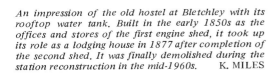
An impression of the old hostel at Bletchley with its rooftop water tank. Built in the early 1850s as the offices and stores of the first engine shed, it took up its role as a lodging house in 1877 after completion of the second shed. It was finally demolished during the station reconstruction in the mid-1960s. K. MILES

In November the following year I took over as Running Foreman at Rowsley and found the situation to be much the same. All the pre-war lodging turns to the north, Stockport, Garston, Longsight, Oldham, etc., had disappeared with the crews on those services being relieved at Buxton, Gowhole or Cheadle. Some of them had originally been reciprocal workings with the foreign crews using private lodgings – with Mrs Cull, for instance, as described in 'Charlie Harrison, Engineman Extraordinary', Journal No.27, or with Mrs. Wall at 'Riverdale'. So, in 1950, the only lodging turns were to the south, London and Bir-

mingham. The London services, for which 'Crabs' had been brought to the shed in the thirties, were at 2.30, class F and 10/5, class E, to Brent Loaded Wagon Sidings, the crews lodging at Cricklewood. From September 1953 Rowsley goods guards also lodged on the morning job. The timetable varied over the years, of course, with the trains being upgraded to E and C respectively and worked by Standard Caprotti Fives from 1959. At one time the morning train went through to St.Pancras Goods with the men lodging at Kentish Town. The hostel there was slightly away from the shed in a side street off Highgate Road, but the

Upper Holloway line ran in a tunnel directly underneath it, causing some disturbance to slumbering locomen. A unique feature of the Kentish Town barracks was the painted gradient profiles of the London – Manchester and Carlisle routes on the walls of the Recreation Room. Applied by the Midland, they survived into BR days. Syd Curzon recalled that, "when the war came along and the rationing began to bite, they stopped the lodging for a bit. On the morning job we'd only go as far as Leicester before being relieved and on the night job it was at Kettering. The same thing happened on the Birmingham job: when they were bombing Birmingham, we'd sometimes get relieved at Burton and lodge – the hostel was at the back of the shed where the brook is." This I can confirm since I visited the building in the 'sixties on a boiler renewal project.

The 1950 Birmingham services, 4F hauled, were the 4.10 class E and the 3/20 class H, both to Washwood Heath with the crews lodging at Saltley. The respective return workings were the 9/20 class E Water Orton – Rowsley and the 2.35 class F Washwood Heath – Brunswick. Most locomen seem to have clearer memories of these services during the war years and I've already shared Saltley goods guard Alf Lovell's comments about the amount of traffic at that time and the resultant congestion in the Birmingham area in 'Aspects of Freight', Journal No.22. Rowsley's Syd Curzon observed that, "The trains used to be solid from Water Orton, just one train after another right into Washwood Heath Sidings." Billy Hodkin went further: "I've been relieved at Water Orton in a morning then gone and lodged. Then we'd come on at night and our train'd still not got into Washwood Heath – you'd get twenty-odd trains, one behind another, stood there. In t'war, if you got an 'air raid red' everything stopped in t'sidings and the trains soon piled up."

Syd remembers one particular incident. "There'd been an air raid, getting dark about five or six o'clock time, and they'd dropped a bomb right on Duddeston Road signal box, killing the signalman. Of course, everything'd come to a stand but we eventually got to Saltley and booked off about ten-something then made our way up to the lodging house. We'd been on duty all that time and we were as black as coal. The only water available was for drinking; they'd done the mains. The water for

The shed yard at Leeds Holbeck, dominated by the LMS No. 1 coaling plant with its two 150-ton bunkers. On the left, 'within fifty yards' (Ken Stokes) is the hostel. Saltley's Bill Alcock had double trips to Leeds in the early 1940s and recalled "There was an old barracks in the depot yard; it had no bathing facilities but at least there was a canteen. We were sometimes allocated sleeping berths in an old camping coach nearby. It was better than the barracks, it was too noisy there."
NRM/COLLECTION K. MILES

Wellingborough in 1959, with the yard full of 8 and 9Fs. On the left is the former Garratt shed (the last was withdrawn from the depot in 1954), with the No. 2 roundhouse beyond. Above its roof can be seen the "not too salubrious hostel with its dubious delights" (Jack Bucken) on Mill Road.
T. WRIGHT, COLLECTION K. MILES

The approach to Primrose Hill tunnels in 1951, and in the background, behind Camden No. 2 signal box, is Camden barracks. "Situated right beside the running lines, including the shunting neck out of busy Camden goods yard, these barracks were reputed to be easily the noisiest of the entire region (Pete Johnson). On my first booking-off trip there, I came to realise this was true enough. Although we had been up early and had worked through part of the night, sleep was almost impossible." E. R. WETHERSETT/COLLECTION R. M. CASSERLEY

washing was in a bucket that they'd been chucking the tealeaves in! This was the option – you either went to bed without having a bit of a clean up; there was no cooking; or make do. It was a case of getting your white cloth and dipping it in the bucket and wiping yourself down." He went on to say, "There were a lot of complaints about Saltley lodging house and I once went to Aston because they reckoned it was a lot better, but it wasn't. Aston barracks was practically right at the side of the track so I wasn't very happy lodging there. Mind you, I wasn't very happy about lodging at all!" It seems that Saltley had gained some notoriety as a 'warm bed barracks', that is to say that crews often had to wait for beds until the previous occupants had been called up out of them. This was partly due, according to Billy, because "a lot of Liverpool lads were living there. Some of them stayed on and eventually became drivers."

Billy also recalled, with some glee, that, "We used to have a job on a Sunday when we used to come on at midnight Saturday night. The engine were already on the train in the Up Sidings and we'd go and relieve it, work to Birmingham and lodge. Then you could come on again when you'd had your time off [nine hours minimum when

booked off away from the home depot] and go light engine to Water Orton. The train were already drawn out on the goods line and you'd back onto it and go when you were ready. I was booked with 'Skipper' Tomlinson or Stan Shimwell at that time and, o'course, their aim was to get back to t'Station Hotel before closing time! You went as hard as you could going, like, so's you could get signed off early, then you could come on early at night. I've been back at eight o'clock on a Sunday night – two days work in one!" By 1960 this job had been compressed into a single trip, enginemen's turn 397 – engine prepared to work the 11/40 SO class E to Washwood Heath, then light engine to Bromford Bridge to turn (there was a turntable just inside the north end of Washwood Heath Up Sidings) and on to Water Orton to work the 4.35 Sun class E to Rowsley, due at 7.0.

Finally, two divergent views on lodging: Grimesthorpe's Ken Stokes said that, "As the firemen moved up the links, they eventually found themselves in the lodging links. One fireman told me that he looked back on his spell in those links as a term of penal servitude." By contrast, Willesden's George Bushell said that, "In the Crewe link there were twenty-two weeks of work and often three weeks and sometimes five weeks of

continuous booking-off turns. Many weeks we would cover thousands of miles on heavy parcels or on fast freights. It was one of the most satisfying periods of my life, even if it seemed detached from normal living, with constant dashing about and spending so much time in lodging houses." I must say that I enjoyed my brief spell on lodging turns at Willesden and Camden but, then, I was young and enthusiastic. However, I was used to being away from home having already spent over three years in digs in Glasgow and was to spend nigh on another five at Crewe and Rowsley before I acquired a wife and a home of my own.

As ever, I'm indebted to those former railwaymen who felt able to record their experiences aurally or in print, my former colleagues at Rowsley and the following:

Ken Stokes, *Both Sides of the Footplate*, Bradford Barton,
George Bushell, *LMS Locoman, Willesden Footplate Memories*, Bradford Barton,
Pete Johnson, *Through the Links at Crewe*, Bradford Barton,
Dick Fawcett, *Ganger, Guard and Signalman*, Bradford Barton,
Peter Brock, *Calling Carlisle Control*, Ian Allan, 1990,
Bill Alcock, *A Locoman's Log, 1937–1985*, Silver Link, 1996.
Jim Backen, *Blowing off Steam*, Silver Link, 1993.

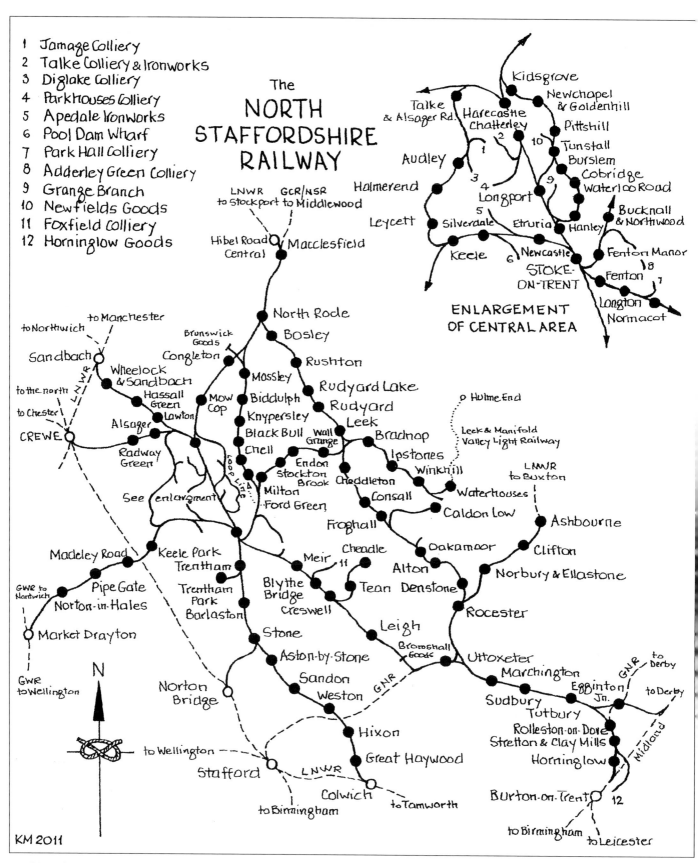

1 Jamage Colliery
2 Talke Colliery & Ironworks
3 Diglake Colliery
4 Parkhouses Colliery
5 Apedale Ironworks
6 Pool Dam Wharf
7 Park Hall Colliery
8 Adderley Green Colliery
9 Grange Branch
10 Newfields Goods
11 Foxfield Colliery
12 Horninglow Goods

The
NORTH
STAFFORDSHIRE
RAILWAY

ENLARGEMENT
OF CENTRAL AREA

KM 2011

Map of the North Staffordshire Railway showing stations, connections with other railways and some of the collieries that helped to provide the traffic carried by the railway.

KNOTTY TALES

by KEITH MILES

Adams Class New C No. 2044 (NSR 173), built 1914, on a southbound local train at Stoke in 1930. The original Class C one-time main-line passenger 2–4–0s of 1874-1884 had been reduced to one by that time and put on the duplicate list as 14A in 1912. These 0–6–4Ts, with 5ft driving wheels and large superheated boilers, were powerful mixed traffic engines.　　　　　J. A. G. H. COLTAS/COLLECTION R. J. ESSERY

The Knotty, of course, was the familiar name widely used with reference to the North Staffordshire Railway. In July 1966, the Victoria Theatre, Stoke-on Trent, presented the first performance of its musical documentary, 'The Knotty', which had been diligently researched over a period of several months including interviews with surviving NSR veterans. It was subsequently revived in 1967, 1969 and 1978 with a special performance for a local businessman and railway enthusiast in 2008. Meantime, however, in 1970, Peter Handford had adapted the work for a record, ARGO ZTR125, using cast members from the theatre company plus the voices of genuine North Staffs railwaymen accompanied by appropriate Transacord sound effects, and I'm fortunate in having had access to a copy. So, as an introduction, here is a broad description of the railway attributed to the long-serving General Manager, W.D. Phillips, based on an interview for the *Railway Magazine* of February 1899.

'It is rather like an octopus with its body in Stoke-on-Trent, stretching out its tentacles in all directions. Northwards to Macclesfield where it joins the London & North Western, northwest to Sandbach and Crewe where again it joins the LNW, westward to Market Drayton where it joins the Great Western, southwards to Norton Bridge and Colwich where again it joins the LNW, and southeast to Burton and Derby where it joins the Midland and Great Northern. 204 miles in all, the longest run from Crewe to Derby being only 51. Most of our runs are so short that the drivers are afraid to put on too much speed for fear of running twenty or thirty miles up somebody else's track before they can stop.'

A bit fanciful, perhaps, but, in fact, the Knotty had running powers over other companies' lines in excess of 300 miles resulting in its stock making unexpected appearances in places far outside the Potteries area. A prime example was the summer-only express service from Derby to Llandudno with $6\frac{1}{2}$ miles on the Midland, $44\frac{1}{2}$ miles on the NSR and $67\frac{1}{2}$ miles on the LNW. Casual passengers were also sometimes surprised to see a tank engine at the head of their London express at Manchester, London Road. This, however, was not an unusual sight for, up to grouping, the 12.10 pm was taken by a Knotty 0–6–4

tank over the $37\frac{1}{2}$ miles to Stoke that included the severe slack around the curve at Cheadle Hulme and a steady climb up to Macclesfield. One of the smaller 0–6–2 tanks banked the train up the 2 miles at 1 in 102 to the Moss, then it was away with its twelve or more coaches down to Stoke where an LNW tender engine was waiting to take over the remainder of the journey to Euston. On one occasion the booked engine developed a defect and the only readily available substitute was one of the 0–6–2Ts, No. 158. This was required to tackle a substantial corridor dining-car train of 310 tons but was driven and fired with such skill that the loss of time to Stockport and Stoke was trifling, near 54 mph being achieved on level track – a remarkable feat. *(Steam Railways of Britain in Colour*, O.S. Nock, Blandford Press, 1967) Otherwise, W.D. Phillips confided that, 'We carry comparatively few passengers, say seven and a half to eight million a year. The number of passenger trains in and out of Stoke station is about 245 each day.'

Freight, however, was a different matter: 'We transport millions of tons of coal, coke and earthenware; china, clay and flints. Beer from Burton amounting to over 225 million gallons a year also passes over our line.' This resulted in a very extended goods network including the twice-daily freight from Derby/Burton to Edge Hill, a daily mineral train from Alsager to Wellingborough and regular workings to such as Edgeley, Manchester, Mold Junction, Rugby and Wellington. This widespread activity required special arrangements by the Locomotive Department. In addition to their own sheds at Stoke (125 engines), Alsager (15), Macclesfield (12), Derby (9), Uttoxeter (8), Burton (7) and Crewe (2), Knotty engines and men were also outstationed at 'foreign' depots: Colwick (1) and Edge Hill, Longsight and Stafford (2 each). Cleaners were included in the staff at Longsight and Stafford and two were also maintained at Wellingborough.

As will be realised from the foregoing, a reciprocal arrangement enabled LNW locomotives to venture onto the Knotty; but first an introduction to Fred Adams: "I left school when I was thirteen and tried the pot works, but I didn't like it. I really wanted to get on the railway and I was pleased as I did because I had such a wonderful life; it was one pleasure. I started on the railway in 1907 when I was sixteen. I went on duty at five o'clock in the morning and finished at four-fourteen at night; that was the early turn. We worked twelve hours – it was twelve hours a day on the railway!" Fred eventually became a passenger guard and recalled that, "You'd got to be careful a'coming up from Kidsgrove to Stoke on the old Loop because there's a bank all the way up [1 in 40 for the first mile and a half] and if you're over-weighted, well, your driver wouldn't make

it. There's a tunnel, what they called Birchenwood; it was the widest tunnel as there was, the widest, I believe, in history. [As far as I'm aware, this tunnel, albeit only 88 yards long, was the only one built to accommodate three tracks; the up and down Loop and a mineral line associated with Birchenwood colliery.] The North Western, they had a train, one o'clock out of London Road, Manchester, and they used to put one of their engines on this train with a big wheel and when it got to this tunnel it was stuck every day nearly. The fireman had to get off and throw cinders on the track; this was well known on the railway. I used to follow him up and get my spade and help them along." However . . .

In the year of nineteen twenty-three
Amalgamation came to be.
Strangers came into the sheds,
Different caps to different heads.

Goodbye to the days of Knotty fame,
Engines bearing drivers' name.
The loss for some was hard to take,
Golden sovereigns hard to make.

Farewell to the world of WD,
Of tip your hat for courtesy.
The personal touch on the personal line,
The NSR was lost to time.

Fred Adams was particularly upset: "When the amalgamation came about, I never dreamt of it 'till it came off all of a sudden. I never gave it an idea, but I didn't like the idea of the Knotty being took over. Y'see in the old Knotty days it was a pleasure, we were all a happy family. The bosses were good, the men and everybody. I didn't think the railway could ever be the same as it was on the old Knotty. Take this station where we are now, (Harecastle, which I knew by its LMS latter day name from October 1944, Kidsgrove Central) there'd come sixty churns of milk up in a van. You used to have to get them out and wheel them onto the Manchester train. There used to be about sixty mailbags from Macclesfield and about forty from Congleton. The porters used to top load them up on barrows and take them across to the Crewe train for Crewe. No, it couldn't be the same; never!" Driver Charles Dawson was slightly more phlegmatic, "When amalgamation came along, Stoke automatically lost a lot of jobs. Derby men collared them, Stafford men collared them, Macclesfield men collared them – y'see, all these outsiders. The Midland and North

NSR LOCOMOTIVES AT GROUPING

Numbers	Class			Built	Designed	Last Wdn
595–599	G&KT	3P	4-4-0	1910-1912	Adams	1933
			Renumbered 5410-5414 1928			
1431-1439	M&NewM	3P	0-4-4T	1907-1920	Adams	1939
1440-1451	B	1P	2-4-0T	1882-1895	Longbottom	1933
1454-1459	A&B	1P	2-4-2T	1898-1901	Longbottom	1934
			Rebuilds of Classes A&B			
1550-1598	D	2F	0-6-0T	1882-1899	Longbottom	1937
1599 (not born)		3F	0-6-0T	1922	Hookham	
			Rebuilt and renumbered 2367 1924			
1600-1601		1F	0-6-0ST	1880-1881	Hudswell Clarke	1933
1602-1603		1F	0-6-0T	1919	Kerr Stuart	1933
2040-2047	New C	5F	0-6-4T	1914-1915	Adams	1937
2048-2055	F	4P	0-6-4T	1916-1919	Adams	1936
2180-2186	K	3P	4-4-2T	1911-1912	Adams	1935
2234-2239	DX	2F	0-6-2T	1899-1902	Longbottom	1931
2240-2273	L&New L	3F	0-6-2T	1903-1923	Adams	1937
			Last four built after grouping			
2320-2342	E	1F	0-6-0	1871-1877	Dodds	1934
			Surviving engines renumbered 8650-8664 1928			
2343-2350	100	2F	0-6-0	1896-1907	Longbottom	1931
2357-2358			Renumbered 8665-8672, 8679-8680 1928			
2351-2356	159	2F	0-6-0	1900	Pettigrew	1936
			Renumbered 8673-8678 1928			
2359-2366	H&NewH	3F	0-6-0	1909-1911	Adams	1930
			Renumbered 8681-8688 1928			
2367	4Cyl.D	3F	0-6-0	Rebuilt 1924	LMS	1928
			Renumbered 8689 1928			

Western collared the jobs and automatically we lost a lot of work. It wasn't an advantage to us; it wasn't promotion, it was like you were being put back a bit. Of course, that's how things run with an amalgamation."

At amalgamation, the North Staffordshire became the fifth largest constituent of the LMS after the enlarged L&NWR, which had amalgamated with the L&Y in 1922, the Midland, Caledonian and G&SW and contributed 196 engines to the locomotive stock as listed in the accompanying table. It will be seen that the Knotty, insofar as passenger work was concerned, had relied on tank engines, possessing only five 4–4–0 tender engines designed for the heavier traffic on the Derby–Crewe line and, in particular, for the summer-only expresses from Derby to Llandudno where they replaced ageing 2–4–0s. These comprised four Adams 1910-designed Class Gs and one Class KT of 1912. The latter was a derivative of his 4–4–2 Class K tanks (LMS 3P) of 1911/12, eight of which were ordered but one was turned out as a tender engine instead. These impressive tank engines were designed specifically for the heavy London-bound restaurant car trains over the hilly route from Manchester to Macclesfield and Stoke and, consequently, had smaller wheels, 6ft, than usual for express work. However, on entering service from 1916, his Class F (LMS 4P) 0–6–4 5ft 6in tanks took over this service, with the possible alternative of the 1914/15 Class C 5ft 0–6–4Ts that he'd designed for the heavier mixed traffic work and that the LMS couldn't decide were to be 5P or 5F – see *Railway Observer* notes on locomotive liveries. Suburban passenger workings were in the hands of a collection of nineteenth century diminutive 2–4–0Ts and their 2–4–2T rebuilds, Classes A and B (1P) plus the more powerful Adams Class M (3P) 0–4–4Ts of 1907 and New M of 1920.

The freight stock numbered 141, comprising 93 tank engines, 47 tender engines and one oddity. The tank engines consisted of 53 0–6–0s including 49 Longbottom Class D of 1882–1899 (the largest single class intact at grouping) and 40 0–6–2s, being half-a-dozen Longbottom Class DX of 1899–1902 and 30 Adams Class L designed in 1903 but with the last four not being completed until after grouping. The tender engines were all 0–6–0s including 23 Dodds veterans of 1871–1877. The remainder were progressively newer classes

Class G 4–4–0 No. 170 (LMS 597/5412) standing in platform 1 at Stoke-on-Trent with a reflection of the overall roof in the upper windows. Above the chimney can be seen the unique extended water crane for use of up trains that was matched by another for down trains at the north end of platform 2. As a sign of the times, visible above the boiler are signs for Ladies First and Third Class Waiting Rooms.   COLLECTION K. MILES

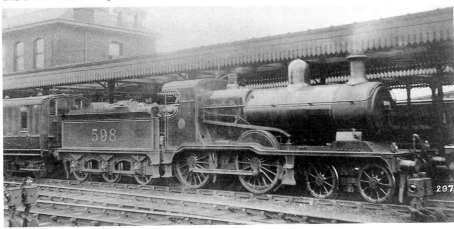

Class G 4–4–0 No. 171 in its early LMS livery as 598 at Stockport, Edgeley. This turned out to be the last of the class, being withdrawn in 1933 as 5413. In their heyday these engines ran the 51 miles from Crewe to Rhyl in 62 minutes on the Derby–Llandudno summer expresses.
COLLECTION K. MILES

LOCOMOTIVE LIVERIES.—Mr. W. T. Stubbs supplies the following notes on North Staffordshire engines :—

0-4-4T " M." Nos. 1435/39 were never painted black, but all others were done in the accepted style except 1436, which was lined out (Oct./Nov. 1934). This is the only N.S. engine ever to be painted in correct passenger livery.

2-4-0T. I believe that 1450 was the only one to be black, and this had the number on the tank.

2-4-2T. All painted black, No. on bunker before scrapping.

" D " 0-6-0T. All these had the 1923-27 style except Nos. 1567/70, which were repainted correctly in 1935. Rather singularly 1583 was repainted a little later but in the 1923-27 style. 1576 remains therefore in the old style, but the red shading behind the " L.M.S." has been painted out.

" C " and " F " 0-6-4T. All were painted in the correct style, although 2046 ran for several years painted black (when all the others were red) but with number on side tanks and a crest on the bunker (as did some L.N.W. 4-6-2 Tanks). Nos. 2040/42/47 were painted 5F instead of 5P and 2051/52/54 4F instead of 4P. This was in 1933, but on 1/12/33 I saw 2047 with 5P chalked over the 5F. I am at a loss to understand how the paint shop at Crewe were misinformed to classify these fine engines wrongly. Also 2054 carried two plates (1914 on air valve and 1919 on splasher) on the same side (left hand) 1934-36.

" K " 4-4-2T were all painted correctly before scrapping.

" L " 0-6-2T. All except 2259 painted correctly. 2259 still has the 1923-27 style complete to the shading behind the " L.M.S." 2252/58 were painted about four years ago with large numbers on the bunker, and an ordinary L.M.S. on the tanks. (2319 was similar, also, I believe, 2322).

Of the G. & K.T. 4-4-0's, only 5413 survived to be painted black, while all the " E " 0-6-0 and " 159 " 0-6-0 scrapped in the last two or three years were in the correct style.

from Longbottom and Adams bolstered by half-a-dozen supplied by Naysmyth-Wilson to a design by Pettigrew originally ordered for the Furness Railway. The odd one out started as one thing and ended up as the other. This was Hookham's experimental 0–6–0T having four cylinders with cranks set at 135 degrees, giving eight exhaust beats per driving wheel revolution. The point of the exercise was an attempt to

find a means of improving suburban passenger services, especially on the steeply-graded lines of the Loop. After some initial problems, the engine seemed quite successful but the LMS would have none of it. It was rebuilt as a tender engine in January 1924, classed '4cyl. D', for local freight trip workings but was withdrawn four years later.

Stoke born and bred railwayman, Allan C. Baker, claims in his *An Illustrated History of Stoke and North Staffordshire's Railways* (Irwell Press, 2000) that the Knotty engines were 'the most modern and well maintained fleet of locomotives, far outweighing any of its contemporaries in their advanced development, size for size.' He also claimed that E.S. Cox had said that it was only the mindless quest of Midlandisation that

Class New M No. 15 built by Hookham in 1920 to Adams' 1907 design, but having longer frames with larger bunkers and water tanks. It became LMS 1436 at the grouping and survived to be the very last North Staffs engine in main-line service when it was withdrawn in April 1939.
F. MOORE'S RAILWAY
PHOTOGRAPHS
COLLECTION K. MILES

No. 1433 (NSR 12), one of the five Adams Class M 0–4–4Ts built in 1907/8 which introduced the new form of cab roof, curving round to join the cab sides in the style then current on the Midland. As with engines all over the LMS system, the original pre-grouping building plate on the front splasher had been replaced by one of the LMS variety.
COLLECTION R. J. ESSERY

Class B 2–4–0 suburban passenger tank No. 2 built by Longbottom to an 1881 Clare design, but fitted with his improved cab. The driver and fireman look satisfied with their steed, Charles Dawson recalling that "There were a lot of old drivers who used to have their own engine, you see. They were very proud of them and everything had to be just to perfection." COLLECTION K. MILES

Class B No. 2 became 2A in 1923 (the NSR, like the Caledonian, was not fully absorbed into the LMS until the July of that year) to make way for one of the New L 0–6–02Ts and is seen here on a local service, possibly near Tutbury. It eventually became LMS 1447 and was withdrawn in 1930. A. G. ELLIS/COLLECTION R. J. ESSERY

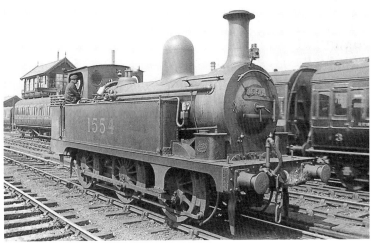

No. 1554 (NSR 37) of Longbottom's numerous Class D 0–6–0Ts, built 1883-1899 with the then standard 4ft dia. boilers, at Stoke in 1930. Having introduced larger boilers on his Class 100 0–6–0s, he initiated the rebuilding of the Ds with 4ft 2in boilers in 1900 and this was continued by Adams up to 1913.
J. A. G. H. COLTAS
COLLECTION R. J. ESSERY

Class D No. 1583 (NSR 138) of 1893 at Crewe Works surrounded by LNW engines, after its withdrawal in 1936. The D was one of the most successful and numerous of all the NSR classes and became the largest single class of NSR locomotives to survive into grouping.
REX CONWAY STEAM RAILWAY COLLECTION

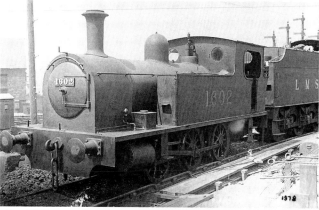

No. 1602, one of the two standard 'Argentina' 0–6–0Ts purchased from neighbouring Kerr, Stuart in 1919 during the difficult post-WW1 period. They were designated Class KS and put to work in Stoke goods yard but with their extended smokeboxes and outside cylinders, they were at odds with all other NSR engines.
F. MOORE'S RAILWAY PHOTOGRAPHS
COLLECTION R. J. ESSERY

The Class F 0–6–4Ts were definitely passenger engines, being designed for express work, in particular the 12.5 p.m. from Manchester, London Road, as far as Stoke. No. 2049 (NSR 4) is here seen on lowlier work at Stoke in May 1932. H. C. CASSERLEY

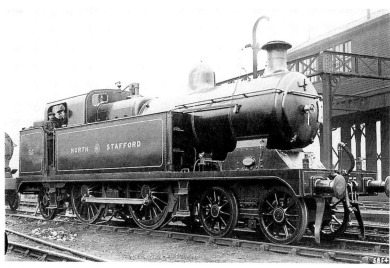

One of the seven impressive Class K 4–4–2 tanks built 1911-1912 for longer-distance passenger services, including the Manchester to Stoke section of the London-bound restaurant car trains. These were basically a superheated version of the Class G 4–4–0s with larger cylinders and piston valves. No. 55 (LMS 2183) is seen at Manchester, London Road.
F. MOORE'S RAILWAY PHOTOGRAPHS
COLLECTION K. MILES

Class K No. 14 (LMS 2185) at the head of a long rake of LNW stock, passing under the striking suspension bridge from Crewe North Junction signal box to the station as it came off the Chester and North Wales line. This was probably not one of the Llandudno trains since tank engines were rarely used, having insufficient coal and water for the outward trip without a stop.
COLLECTION R. J. ESSERY

Again possibly at Tutbury c.1920, Class DX 0–6–2T No. 27 (LMS 2239) heading a train of mixed vans and wagons past a works siding holding two coal wagons from Moira Colliery, Ashby-de-la-Zouch. The half-dozen DXs were the smallest of the 0–6–2Ts being enlargements of the Ds with longer fireboxes and railed bunkers over a radial truck.
COLLECTION R. J. ESSERY

Class L 0–6–2T No. 2244 (NSR 167) at Stoke shed, one of the six built by Vulcan Foundry in 1903. These had been the first engines to receive Adams' new livery of Madder Lake, lined out in yellow and vermilion, replacing Longbottom's Victoria Brown.
REAL PHOTOGRAPHS COLLECTION R. J. ESSERY

Adams introduced eight New Ls with saturated boilers in 1908/9 having the new cab roofs and higher bunker sides, and eight more followed in 1913. Hookham built a further eight in 1920/21 but with one of them fitted with a superheated boiler. A series of trials ensued, resulting in four more superheated engines being ordered but not delivered until 1923, as shown here by 2270 (NSR 1) at Crewe South in 1929.
H. C. CASSERLEY

On taking over as Company Engineer in 1870, Thomas Dodds found that the most urgent need was for goods engines and built two 0–6–0s at Stoke in 1871. These were followed by ten from Vulcan Foundry in 1872, eight from Sharp, Stewart in 1873/4, six from Beyer Peacock in 1874 and a final four from Stoke in Clare's time, 1875–77. These were all later to be designated Class E. Here is Beyer Peacock-built No. 119 in its later guise from 1918 as 119A (LMS 2335).

A. G. ELLIS/COLLECTION R. J. ESSERY

Below: Longbottom Class 100 No. 8666 (NSR 78) on Target 104 at Stoke in 1930. Eight of these engines were built between 1896 and 1900, the first class to have the 4ft 2in boilers. The comprehensive rebuilding programme then taking place at Stoke Works halted further deliveries and, as an interim measure, six engines intended for the Furness Railway were purchased from Nasmyth-Wilson, the Class 159. However, two more modified Class 100s were later added by Adams in 1907, differing in appearance by the abandonment of the rectangular lower cabside panels.

J. A. G. H. COLTAS/COLLECTION R. J. ESSERY

The odd one out – the Hookham 4-cylinder experimental engine first built as an 0–6–0T – see insert. Nonetheless, the LMS were not enamoured with it and rebuilt it as a tender engine in 1924, changing its number from 1599 (NSR 23) to 2367. It is seen here in Stoke goods yard during its brief life as a trip engine until its withdrawal in 1928. COLLECTION R. J. ESSERY

WILLS'S CIGARETTES.

From a set of fifty cigarette cards issued by W. D. & H. O. Wills, 1923-24.

prevented the later Class L 0–6–2T becoming an early LMS standard, although it should be said that I cannot find any evidence to support it. It was inevitable, therefore, that due to the wide variety of classes and lack of standardisation 'this modern fleet of soundly designed, easy to maintain, robust and much-loved locomotive' followed the same fate as that of the G&SW and all were withdrawn in the 1930s, the last to go being Class New M 0–4–4T 1436 in April 1939.

It seems, by the way, that engine trouble on the Loop was not confined to pre-grouping days. Ken Jackson of the Permanent Way Department recalled that, 'They used to send these big engines round the Loop, the LMS did. Well, they weren't built for the job and the Loop Line wouldn't take them. We had no end of derailments with these big engines. They used to come off, the curves were too sharp for them, see. Well, these little locos that the Knotty built were built specially for the track. There's a lot of sharp curves on the Loop, you know, and they'd send these engines with a big wheel base and they wouldn't go round the curves. When they sent these engines and they came off, we used to say, 'Send for a Knotty, that'll shift it', and it did!" Seemingly, it was eventually decided that that the Class 5 was the largest engine to be allowed. That was not the end of the trouble, however, since it was discovered that BR Standard Mark 1 coaching stock would not pass through the platforms at Hanley! Passenger services on the Loop finally ceased in March 1964.

Apart from a brief visit to Stoke shed in 1947, my first real contact with the Knotty came about in 1949 while an Improver at Willesden, 'firing on locomotives in service as third man.' It was a lodging job – engine-

men's turns 800/802, the 9.50 pm FF2 Camden–Adswood, returning on the 9.20 pm FF2 Stockport–Willesden (the new BR train classifications didn't come in until June 1950) with a Black Five in each direction. On the outward trip with 50 on including 22 fitted, a stop was made at Stoke in the early hours for train examination. In my mind's eye I can still see the atmospheric scene of the bobbing lamp of the examiner as he moved up the train in the steamy darkness, and hear the tap of his hammer on the wheels. On the return journey, a stop was made at Kidsgrove Central to take water. The fireman climbed onto the tender back to put in the bag, then called down to me to turn on the water. I tugged at the control wheel but, as hard as I tried, it wouldn't budge. Hearing the resultant exasperated comments from the fireman, the driver got down and turned the wheel with no trouble at all but he turned it clockwise! The hand-wheel of any other column that I'd come across (or any other valve for that matter) was at one with the spindle and both rose together as the wheel was turned anti-clockwise to open the valve. In the gloom I hadn't noticed that, for once, the spindle was threaded and the wheel was captive on the valve bonnet. Turning it clockwise drew the spindle up through its centre and opened the valve.

Fortunately, the darkness hid my embarrassment but the driver and fireman were amused.

Years later, in the Chief Civil Engineer's Department, I was involved on several sites at Stoke: Cockshute Carriage Sidings and the short-lived DMU Depot (1957–1966), the station itself including the Divisional Manager's Office plus the Power Signal Box, the Plant & Machinery Depot and Glebe Street S&T Depot. I also took part in the 1979 refurbishment of Stone Station. There the architect was persuaded to open up one of the sealed chimneys for my boiler, and his model-makers' section provided a large decorative fibreglass pot to match all the others on the building. In 1969, during the construction of a new Wagon Repair Depot at Burton, hard by the North Stafford Junction signal box, I took the opportunity of exploring the nearby Horninglow station. To my astonishment, I found it just as the last porter must have left it when he locked the doors behind him on closure twenty years earlier in January 1949. However, C.J. Gammell reported in his 1991 *LMS Branch Lines* that only 'the rotting remains can still be seen.' From 1997 I attended the twice-yearly Bakewell Reunions for former LMS staff in the grandeur of the one-time railway North Stafford Hotel opposite Stoke station

An overall view of Stoke engine shed from the north in July 1936. The left-hand portion had losts its roof the year before and a start was made to re-roof it in 1938, but work was suspended at the outbreak of war. Completion of the scheme in the BR style was not achieved until the early 1950s. Several Class L 0—6—2Ts are visible, including 2257 in the foreground, and over on the right is Class D No. 1597 with the old style cab. When I visited the shed in 1947, I found two LNW 'Cauliflowers' present. I've discovered since that they had been introduced after all the Knotty engines had been scrapped in order to work the Newfield Branch.

W. L. GOOD/COLLECTION R. J. ESSERY

out, sadly, since 2003, these have removed to a less sumptuous venue at Crewe.

Sources of information other than those mentioned in the text include: *The North Staffordshire Railway*, Rex Christiansen & Bob Miller, David & Charles, 1971, and the New Victoria Theatre programme for the November 2008 performance of 'The Knotty.' I'm also grateful to the theatre management for permission to 'make reference to and quote from the production'.

A tree-less vista of Milton Junction on the Biddulph Valley line in 1959, the branch off to the right leading to Leek Brook Junction. The skyline is dominated by colliery tips and iron works slag heaps. Passenger services beyond Milton Junction to Biddulph ceased in 1927, the first North Staffs branch line passenger service to close under the LMS.

NORTH STAFFORDSHIRE RAILWAY

NOTICE IS HEREBY GIVEN THAT ANY PERSON WHO SHALL TRESPASS UPON ANY OF THE RAILWAYS OF THE COMPANY IN SUCH A MANNER AS TO EXPOSE HIMSELF TO DANGER OR RISK OF DANGER THEREBY RENDERS HIMSELF LIABLE TO A PENALTY NOT EXCEEDING **FORTY SHILLINGS** OR IN DEFAULT ONE MONTH'S **IMPRISONMENT**

BY ORDER

We conclude with this picture of a North Staffordshire Railway Trespass Board. Forty shillings in those days could be several weeks wages.

This picture, taken from the Hanley to Newcastle road, shows the down side of the platform, with the down goods line just visible in the lower right-hand corner. Note the signal arm for the Loop Line had been removed.

ETRURIA

We continue the North Staffordshire Railway theme from the previous article by Keith Miles with a brief look at Etruria. My wife was born in Newcastle-under-Lyme and although we lived in Hemel Hempstead, it was not unusual to spend weekends with her parents, which gave me the opportunity of taking pictures of the local railway scene. These pictures of Etruria were taken during the late summer of 1964, but as a result of refiling my negatives, the precise date is not known, although almost certainly it would have been on a Sunday.

The passenger station at Etruria was north of Stoke-on-Trent, between Newcastle Junction, where the line to Newcastle-under-Lyme diverged to the west, and Etruria Junction where it diverged to the east and marked the beginning of the Loop Line (see accompanying map of the area). Etruria station was on an island platform with Etruria Junction signal box on the opposite side of the bridge. There were four running lines; the inner lines ran alongside the platform with up and down goods lines outside of the passenger lines. On the Stoke side of the station, on the down side of the line, there were private sidings serving Hall Lewis & Co. and Wengers Ltd., a large ceramic, colour and chemical manufacturer, whilst to the north there was Etruria yard and Grange Sidings, just two of the various groups of sidings in the area.

The station entrance from the Hanley to Newcastle Road led passengers down a covered walk-way to platform level, where I found the unusual high-backed double-sided wooden seat below.

The map of the central area of the North Staffordshire Railway, to be read in conjunction with the map on page 10. Reproduced from The North Staffordshire Railway *by Rex Christiansen and R. W. Miller.*

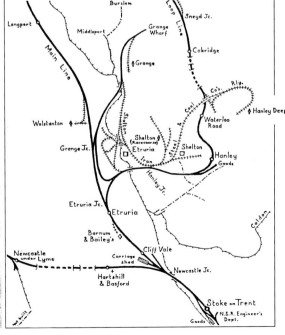

A hundred Compounds were bought from the trade including No. 1138 which was built by the North British Locomotive Company in July 1925 as part of Lot 18, which numbered 25 engines. The other 75 were from Vulcan Foundry which, like the North British Locomotive Company, was to feature strongly in the trade purchases by the LMS during the 1930s.
COLLECTION JOHN JENNISON

Locomotive Purchases from the 'Trade'

by JOHN JENNISON

The LMS purchased almost 1,500 locomotives from private builders between 1923 and 1942 and the background to these orders provides a fascinating insight into the business and economic climate in which the railway operated. Its position as the largest joint-stock company in the world gave it significant economic 'clout' but at the same time made it an obvious target for those whose interests were at variance from it. Matters came to a head in the mid-1930s as the country came out of the Depression years and the private locomotive manufacturing businesses struggled in the face of a steadily declining export market. Inevitably they turned to the home railway companies in an attempt to replace the lost business. The Locomotive Manufacturers' Association, a body representing the builders and which received a $\frac{1}{2}$% levy on all orders, was at the centre of much of the debate. The Government, represented by the Board of Trade, was also involved in measures to counter unemployment by providing financial assistance.

An LMS internal memo set the scene:

ROLLING STOCK INDUSTRY

For some years the railway companies have suffered attacks in regard to their policy of placing orders for their rolling stock requirements.

The most impudent one was by Counsel opposing the London Passenger Transport Bill, who informed the Parliamentary Committee in 1931 that a foreign or overseas buyer wishing to buy locomotives here cannot be taken by a manufacturer and shewn "the performance of a locomotive built by them on a British railway". That was challenged and repudiated (privately only) by those instructing him.

In April 1933, Lord Dudley raised the question in the House of Lords and the Government spokesman replied suggesting that the parties should discuss rationalisation together. The Minister of Transport asked for the railway observations and was informed that the companies would discuss the question if the manufacturers desired.

In September of that year the *Daily Express* stated that the railways did not charge all proper costs to locomotive construction, and in October 1933, Mr Dabell the Secretary of the Locomotive Association wrote to the press on the increasing menace of railway policy, stating that the trade were 'lacking the support of the railways who had gradually turned their essential repair shops into huge establishments devoted to new construction and the trade of the builders for some years had been over 90% export'.

The *Daily Telegraph* in the same month in a special article quoting Mr Dabell said that the four railway companies build practically the whole of their engine requirements and cater for the smaller lines which they absorbed. These are merely samples of the stream of criticism which appears to be trade inspired and has lately been revived.

The allegations are two:−

(1) Railways have curtailed their orders.
(2) Railway costs are untrue.

Neither statement is correct.
As regards the L.M.S. alone the facts are:−

(1) A greater part of its diminished requirements has gone to the trade in post-war than in prewar years.
(2) They have stopped construction at all but two shops and have restricted production there since amalgamation, with considerable staff and local authority complaints and even litigation.
(3) The object was to assist the Home trades in a time of difficulty, and they have gone far in that direction, knowing the value of Home orders to the trade in spreading standing costs and keeping their works going at a time of scarcity of orders.

(4) Railway costs are generally lower than outside prices, not due in *all* cases to better organisation but mainly to the fact that repair work and construction work balance operations and permit *each* to be more economical. This despite the fact that L.M.S. shop costs had no derating benefit.

That had been explained more than once by the Chairman at the annual meetings of the company, despite attacks from shareholders on placing orders outside, and by evidence of the company's officers in the Law Courts.

With this position it is naturally an annoyance, to put it mildly, to have a series of untrue statements which by their nature must relate, amongst others, to the L.M.S. Company, who could with economy perform all their locomotive construction work. In no case do the Association appear to have contradicted these mis-statements.

The recent resumption of press propaganda if not inspired by the Trade (and their assurance is accepted) obviously emanated from someone with a knowledge of the Association memorandum to the Board of Trade, which appears to have many features in common with the previous criticisms of railway policy.

So far the railway companies have made no direct reply to these allegations although (without reference to the Association or a member of it) incidentally the economy of the L.M.S. Company's arrangements has been justified in the Courts and elsewhere.

These representations to the President of the Board of Trade if not modified call for a rejoinder from the company which will set out the actual position; pre-war and since amalgamation, e.g.

(1) The origin of railway construction work nearly 100 years ago
(2) A like controversy in 1867 and the report of the L.N.W Company's auditors that manufacture of 256 locomotives saved that company £150,000.
(3) The economy of a comprehensive lay-out of the shops in order to manufacture locomotive parts for repairs, partial renewals and construction of new units, together with the design of the shops for repair and erection work in order to secure a steady flow of work and economic use of the locomotives and shops. This economy is secured notwithstanding the fact that there is no derating credit as outside and higher rates of wages are paid.
(4) The undue rise in builders' prices after the War, and the consequent need to lay out the chief railway shops to provide for all their requirements, if necessary.
(5) The subsequent stoppage of building work at Inverness, Kilmarnock, St. Rollox, Barrow, Stoke and Horwich
   and
   Concentration of building work at Crewe and Derby with a policy of working plant on a moderate scale for part requirements only, provided reasonable prices were quoted for remaining requirements. (In considering reasonable prices regard is had to all costs plus profit).
(6) The actual work offered to the trade, the prime reasons why traders were not accepted in a few cases and the comparative actual outlay on the work thus transferred to shop construction.
(7) The actual contracts for trade orders for complete locomotives each year.
(8) The growth and not the decline in the trade-built proportion of L.M.S. stock.
(9) The statutory obligation on the company to shew economy in its arrangements, and the economy of their locomotive manufactures. This is illustrated by the closing of the shops mentioned above (5) and concentration at two centres in place of eight.
(10) Their reply to the Minister of Transport on Lord Dudley's proposals.

Before making any such representations this opportunity is welcomed of hearing what the Association have to say and whether they propose to correct their representations to the Board of Trade.

There is one further matter, quite apart from the Board of Trade representations.

No. 4352, built by Kerr Stuart in May 1927, was one of over 150 4F 0–6–0s built by four different outside firms between 1924 and 1928, following the fifty built by Armstrong Whitworth for the Midland Railway in 1921/22. The fifty engines of this class were the only locomotives produced by this builder for the LMS and were delivered in two lots, Nos. 4082-4106 in 1925 and 4332-4356 in 1926/27.
COLLECTION JOHN JENNISON

The Standard Class 3F 0–6–0Ts were second only to the Class 5 4–6–0s in the numbers purchased from outside manufacturers. Four hundred 'Jinties' were ordered by the LMS from five different builders together with a further five by the Somerset & Dorset Joint Railway. No. 16624, which came into service in May 1928, was one of 90 from Wm. Beardmore & Co. and was the last engine of the first batch, Nos. 16600-24, with the second lot of 65 locomotives, 16685-16749, arriving in 1928/9.

It is clearly difficult for the company to have trading relations with those who allege that they are either ignorant of their costs or ignore their implications. The company are willing, as they always have been, to discuss any question the Trade may wish to raise, including an exchange of costs with a mutual examination of detail figures for particular orders.

The recent type of outside criticism of and mis-statement of their policy cannot continue side by side with trading relations. If the placing of orders, when there is scope for these, has a sequence complaint of unfair or improper treatment when there is no scope for orders, the obvious remedy is not to place any more outside orders. Apart from this the company will not submit to any suggestion that any orders, however financed, must be placed outside. To any such suggestion they must apply the commonsense test of reasonableness of the alternative means. They made proposals to the Government several months ago for special financing of a special locomotive programme which it was intended to place outside but only if prices quoted were appropriate to cost conditions.

The LMS as the largest of the four companies took all of this very seriously and the Chairman, Sir Josiah Stamp, was personally involved in the discussions which took place. The background papers which were prepared for him by his officers summarise not only the purchasing 'from the trade' by all of the railway companies and the LMS in particular, but give some interesting details of the orders placed by the company and the tendering process which determined where certain classes were eventually built.

Memo to the Chairman from W.V. Wood on 15th January 1936 titled Locomotive Purchases

With reference to our conversation last Friday morning, I attach a memorandum setting out fairly fully the purchases of recent years, together with a short summary of the net figures.

Perhaps you will say whether this is sufficiently complete for your purpose or whether there is any further information you would like extracted.

CONTRACTS FOR SUPPLY OF STEAM LOCOMOTIVES

The general policy of the company in placing orders with locomotive manufacturers for supplies of locomotives is to call for tenders from British builders. There are occasional exceptions in regard to specialities of particular builders, e.g., 30 'Garratt' locomotives ordered from Beyer Peacock & Co. Ltd. In 1930 and in December 1926, an order was placed with the North British Locomotive Co. Ltd, for the first 50 of the 'Royal Scot' type after negotiations on prices with them alone. Since then all orders have been placed after tenders from builders.

The L.M.S. Company's purchases from the Trade since the War included:–

Builder	Total	Royal Scot	4F 0–6–0	0–6–0T	Compound	Other	Notes
Vulcan Foundry	195			120	75		
North British Loco.	231	51	80	75	25		Includes 6399 Fury
Hunslet	90			90			
Nasmyth Wilson	15					15	5 3P 4–4–2T and 10 2P 0–4–4T
W.G. Bagnall	30			30			Includes 5 built for the SDJR
Andrew Barclay & Sons	25		25				
Beyer Peacock	33					33	33 Beyer-Garratt
Kitson & Co	5					5	5 0F 0–4–0ST
Armstrong Whitworth	55		55				Includes 5 built for the SDJR
Robert Stephenson & Co	5					5	5 2–8–0s built for SDJR
Kerr Stuart	50		50				
Beardmore	91			90		1	Prince of Wales 4–6–0
	825	51	210	405	100	59	

The background information supplied to Stamp also included an analysis of the locomotive stock:–

LOCOMOTIVE STOCK – PURCHASED AND BUILT BY LMS RAILWAY COMPANY

	Purchased		Built in Company's shops		
Date of stock	Number	% of total stock	Number	% of total stock	TOTAL STOCK
1st January 1923	3,029	29.36%	7,287	70.64%	10,316
31st December 1929	3,100	31.63%	6,700	68.37%	9,800
31st December 1934	2,410	30.11%	5,594	69.89%	8,004

From To	Number	% of total stock	Number	% of total stock	TOTAL STOCK
Year 1913	27	17.65%	126	82.35%	153
1st January 1923 – 31st December 1929	744	43.38%	971	56.62%	1,715
1st January 1923 – 31st December 1932	784	36.16%	1,384	63.84%	2,168
1st January 1923 – 31st December 1934	875	35.45%	1,593	64.55%	2,468
1st January 1923 – 31st December 1936 (1)	1,065	35.96%	1,897	64.04%	2,962
1st January 1923 – 31st December 1936 (2)	1,434	42.79%	1,917	57.21%	3,351

(1) to completion of authorised works
(2) to completion of authorised works and proposed loan scheme

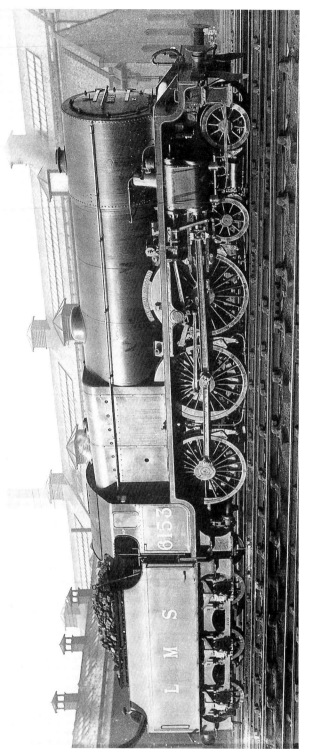

The final twenty Royal Scot 4-6-0s, Nos. 6150-6169 delivered in 1930, would have been expected to be built by the North British Locomotive Company as a follow-on from the original fifty they produced in 1927. However, the LMS decided to build them at Derby instead, because North British quoted a price of £300 more per locomotive compared to the earlier batch, which they deemed excessive because North British already had the necessary patterns and tools. This contrasts sharply with the 1926 order when the LMS was desperate to get its new express design into service and then North British were the only firm asked to quote, and illustrates the dramatically different conditions prevailing by the end of the decade.

COLLECTION R. J. ESSERY

The Jubilees were the first Stanier design to be built by the trade, and the North British Locomotive Company's quote of £5,710 per locomotive and tender was the lowest, with the highest of eight submissions coming in at no less then £7,400. As with the Royal Scots, the order of 50 engines was shared between the two North British works in Glasgow; No. 5560 was built at the Hyde Park site and is shown here at Crewe soon after delivery in July 1934. In that same month, quotes were obtained from ten firms for more of the 3-cylinder 4-6-0s and the lowest tender of £5,813 was that of Armstrong Whitworth and Company. However, in the meantime, a further fifty Class 5s had been ordered from them and thus the delivery time would not be acceptable to the LMS. The next lowest price was from North British at £6,075, which was £365 more than that tendered by them in the previous November for the first fifty. This price was considered too high in relation to the 1933 prices and those in the Company's shops and so the engines were built in-house.

L. HANSON

BUILT NORTH BRITISH LOCO 1934. W/DRN. 1963. (LATER NAMED "PRINCE EDWARD ISLAND") CARNFORTH 1937, HOLBECK 1942. (FORMERLY 5560.)

Figures for the other group companies reflected the pattern of the LMS with trade orders coming to an end as the railways struggled in the Depression years of the early 1930s.

New Locomotives – Four Group Companies 1923–34

Year	Built	Purchased	Total	% purchased
1923	232	10	242	4.1%
1924	222	188	410	45.9%
1925	357	260	617	42.1%
1926	372	201	573	35.1%
1927	374	290	664	43.7%
1928	364	297	661	44.9%
1929	412	129	541	23.8%
1930	321	183	504	36.3%
1931	293	85	378	22.5%
1932	263	6	269	2.2%
1933	219	1	220	0.5%
1934	288	103	391	26.3%
	3,717	1,753	5,470	32.0%

The Minutes of the LMS Board and its sub-committees recorded and authorised each of these purchases and it is apparent that after the completion of the large-scale orders for the new standard designs in the late 1920s (4Fs, Jinties and Compounds) that the tap was turned off as the wider economic situation began to bite. This is well illustrated by the decision to build the final batch of Royal Scots at Derby rather than to buy more from the original supplier:-

Memo January 1936

ROLLING STOCK PRICES – LOCOMOTIVES

In December 1926 the North British Locomotive Company tendered for fifty 4-6-0 'Royal Scot' locomotives at a price of £7,725, and an order was placed accordingly. No other firm was invited to tender.

In January 1930 we required a further twenty of these locomotives, and having regard to the repetitive nature of the work the North British Locomotive Company only were asked to tender. They quoted a price of £8,175 which, after negotiation, was reduced to £8,025. Having regard to the drop in prices 1927–1931 and that the firm possessed dies, blocks, and patterns, the cost of which would be incurred in respect of their previous order, the increase in price of £300 was considered unreasonable and the order was placed on the L.M.S. workshops.

	£
Total estimated Departmental cost of Building as shown in Minute 1030, June 1930	154,800
Total actual Departmental cost	147,494
Actual less than estimate	7,306

The overall comparative adjusted costs of purchase from Contractors and Building in Company's Shops were:–

	Variable (Out-of-pocket)	Non-Variable (Constant)*	TOTAL
Purchase	161,705		161,705
Building in Company's Shops	129,367	36,760	166,127
	32,338		
		36,760	4,422

*Including Interest

The building in the Company's shops resulted in an economy of £32,338, but the overall cost of building exceeded the Contractor's price by £4,422.

The differential in the costs being:–

	£
Wages – Extra cost of higher wage rate of 6/6d paid to Company's employees	6,618
Rates – Relief of 75% given to Contractors	499
Patterns etc – Already possessed by Contractors	180
TOTAL	7,297

The price and cost of each locomotive were:–

		£
Purchase		
Contract Price		8,025
Extras		50
Inspection		10
		8,085

Building	Per cent of Total	
Wages	27.6%	2,296
Materials purchased	38.2%	3,174
Workshop Expenses	21.8%	1,808
Superintendence	3.0%	247
National Insurance and Workmen's Compensation	0.9%	78
Rates	0.4%	33
Maintenance of Buildings	1.1%	92
Direction & Management	2.2%	179
Carriage on Coal & Coke	0.3%	27
Interest @ 5.5% on Floating Capital and Fixed Assets	4.5%	372
	100.0%	8,306

EXCESS COST OF BUILDING (after allowing for full contribution to Constant Overheads) £221

Differential items in the cost:–	
Higher Wages	331
Higher Rates	25
Patterns, etc	9
	£365

The Variable (out-of-pocket) costs were 78% and the Non-Variable (constant) costs were 22% of the total cost

Stanier Class 5 4–6–0 No. 5033 was built at Vulcan Foundry in September 1934, but if the lowest quote for the first batch of the class had been accepted, it would have been delivered from North British Locomotive Company. Their price was £55 lower per locomotive and tender than Vulcan's but the LMS needed the engines urgently and therefore divided the concurrent work on fifty Jubilees and fifty Class 5s between the two builders to obtain a quicker delivery. When quotes were invited for further locomotives in July 1934, Vulcan were undercut by Armstrong Whitworth whose price of £5,343 was around £300 lower, and after some investigation of the bid, 100 engines and tenders were ordered from them. Fifty more were offered to the next lowest builder, North British Locomotive Company, at £5,500, which was £290 below their tender, but they declined and the order went instead to Vulcan Foundry.

COLLECTION JOHN JENNISON

After Stanier arrived from the Great Western in January 1932, the LMS embarked on a major programme to modernise its locomotive stock. Large numbers of his new designs were required urgently, and trade prices were sought for the quantity production of what became the Jubilee and Class 5 4–6–0s:

In November, 1933 tenders were invited for 4–6–0 2-cylinder and 3-cylinder locomotives and tenders, in lots of 25 or 50. Eight different firms tendered for the 2-cylinder type, lots of 25, at prices ranging from £5,625 to £6,900, and four of these also tendered for lots of 50 at prices ranging from £5,485 to £6,795. The same firms tendered for the 3-cylinder type at prices ranging from £5,810 to £7,525 for lots of 25, and from £5,710 to £7,400 for lots of 50.

50 of each type were ordered –

50 3-cylinder from North British Co. Ltd. at   £5,710 each
50 2-cylinder from Vulcan Foundry Co. Ltd. at   £5,540 each

the latter price was £55 in excess of the North British Company's tender but was accepted owing to better deliveries obtainable by dividing the work.

In July, 1934, tenders were obtained from ten firms for further supplies of both of the types ordered in 1933, the quotations being–

	20	30	50
3-cylinder	£5,879 to £7,220	£5,843/7,180	£5,813/7,150
2-cylinder	£5,428 to £6,575	£5,395/6,575	—

The size of the orders put the LMS in a position to drive a hard bargain and, as with the Royal Scots in 1930, they would not pay what they believed to be excessive prices when ordering additional batches of existing designs. Coincidentally, the same supplier was involved:–

The lowest tender for fifty 4–6–0 three-cylinder locomotives was that of Messrs. Armstrong Whitworth and Company, from whom fifty mixed traffic locomotives were being ordered and consequently the period of delivery would not be satisfactory. The next tender in order of merit was that of the North British Locomotive Company at £6,075. This was £365 more than that (£5,710) tendered in the previous November for fifty. Having regard to the fact that the cost of patterns, tools, dies and blocks would have been incurred in respect of the previous locomotives, the price of £6,075 was considered unreasonable and the order was placed on the L.M.S. workshops.

The 2-cylinder type price, on the other hand, was appreciably lower, for one firm, than that of 1933, but as in the meantime further special requirements of this type were under consideration, it was decided to re-tender for

it in lots of 50, 75, 100 and 150. The new tenders were received from each of the ten firms in August, 1934, the quotations being:-

50	75	100	150
£5,365/6,575	£5,353/6,350	£5,343/6,350	£5,335/6,350

The lowest price for each number in both the July and August tenders was from Armstrong Whitworth and Co. Ltd. who had received no orders for locomotives since 1922, and had in the meantime undergone extensive re-organisation. Their prices being much lower than those of other firms, they were informed that before discussing orders the company required to be satisfied:-

(1) that their tender was not based on an unremunerative cut price,
(2) that no question of extras arose,
(3) that their facilities and inspection arrangements were adequate.

Recent work done by the firm for another railway company settled the second and third points, and an examination of their costs the first one.

The five lowest tenders were then considered. These were:-

	For 50	For 100
Armstrong Whitworth & Co Ltd	£5,365	£5,343
R. Stephenson & Co	£5,600	did not tender
Vulcan Foundry Ltd	£5,668	£5,608
Hawthorn Leslie & Co	£5,770	did not tender
North British Locomotive Co.	£5,790	£5,790

and it was decided to order 100 from Armstrong Whitworth at £5,343 and 50 from other firms.

Their deliveries were:-

	20 weeks	30 weeks	50 weeks
R. Stephenson & Co	41	49	65
Vulcan Foundry Ltd	22	25	32
Hawthorn Leslie & Co	56	69	95
North British Locomotive Co.	37	42	36

and it was decided to offer 25 each to Vulcan Foundry Ltd. and North British Locomotive Co. at the price of £5,500, or £168 and £290 respectively below their tenders. In the meantime, Beyer Peacock & Co. Ltd. who had tendered at £6,550 (20), £6,525 (30) and £6,400 (50) pressed their claim, but it was considered that their tender ruled them out of consideration. The North British Company refused the offer and the Vulcan Foundry Company who were next seen agreed to supply 50 at £5,500.

The savings made were appreciable even between the most competitive tenders as the Company used its purchasing muscle to obtain the lowest prices:–

STEAM LOCOMOTIVES – PURCHASES FROM TRADE – 1933 TO 1935.

Year	Description	Firm	Orders actually placed			Cost if orders had been placed with nearest alternative tenderer			Difference between accepted tender and nearest alternative tender	
			Number	Price	Amount	Firm	Price	Amount	Price	Amount
				£	£		£	£	£	£
1933	4–6–0 2 cylr.	VF	50	5,540	277,000	NBL (A)	5,485	274,250	–55	–2,750
	4–6–0 3 cylr.	NBL	50	5,710	285,500	VF (A)	5,834	291,700	124	6,200
					562,500			565,950		3,450
1934	4–6–0 2 cylr.	AW	100	5,343	534,300	VF (B)	5,608	560,800	265	26,500
	4–6–0 2 cylr.	VF	50	5,500	275,000	RS	5,600	280,000	100	5,000
					809,300			840,800		31,500
1935	4–6–0 2 cylr.	AW	227	6,080	1,380,160	VF	6,165	1,399,455	85	19,295
	2–8–0 Freight	VF	69	6,446	444,774	BP	6,450	445,050	4	276
	2–6–4 Tank	NBL	73	5,615	409,895	RS (C)	5,595	408,435	–20	–1,460
					2,234,829			2,252,940		18,111
			619		£3,606,629			£3,659,690		£53,061

NOTES
A   The most economical cost would have been realised (£2,750) by placing both orders with the North British Locomotive Co. but the locomotives were urgently required, and we got delivery in 37 and 49 weeks respectively, whereas if the NBL had got both orders the delivery would have extended over 54 weeks.
B   The Vulcan Foundry Company's price was eventually reduced to £5,500 but as this reduction was mainly due to the low price of £5,343 tendered by Armstrong Whitworth and Co., presumably no case would have arisen for insisting on a reduction if Armstrong Whitworth and Co. had not tendered.
C   Deliveries would not have been completed until September 1937 compared with August 1936 by the North British Locomotive Company.

In the mid-1930s the Government introduced large-scale support for the British manufacturing sector in an effort to stimulate economic activity and the LMS was to take full advantage of the favourable financial terms available by ordering over £2.5 million of new locomotives from the Trade for delivery in 1936/7. However, this took place against a gathering storm in the press against the railway companies. Having recently placed orders of a significant amount and with even more in prospect, it is not difficult to see why Stamp and his Board took offence with what we might nowadays call a media campaign in late 1935 against the railways by the locomotive trade. Whether it was instigated by one or more of the 'losers' in the tendering process or by the industry in general is unclear, but the extent of the press coverage must have given rise to considerable activity at LMS headquarters to counteract the 'spin'. The following summaries were prepared for Stamp and his executives on the press activity.

YORKSHIRE POST 18th OCTOBER, 1935
ARTICLE ON BRITISH LOCOMOTIVE INDUSTRY
Under the heading
'BRITISH LOCOMOTIVE INDUSTRY
Rapid Exhaustion of Capital Resources
APPEAL TO GOVERNMENT'

POINTS

(1) Representations are being made by the Locomotive Manufacturer's Association to President of the Board of Trade, asking Government to bring influence on railway companies to curtail their own construction and put out more work to private builders.
(2) Capital represented by industry is £7,250,000 with an annual production capacity of 1,900 modern locomotives and an estimated employment of 23,000 men.
(3) To-day employment is possible for only 9,069 men due to ruthless competition from abroad aided by Government subsidies and lack of adequate support from home railways.
(4) British railways now produce practically all their own locomotives.
(5) Only on occasions of emergency that locomotives are put out to contract by open competition.
(6) Railway companies, it is estimated, are building up to one third of the total productive capacity of the country, representing a value of £2,000,000.

YORKSHIRE POST 22nd OCTOBER, 1935
ARTICLE ON BRITISH LOCOMOTIVE INDUSTRY
Under the heading
'ENGINE BUILDERS' DIFFICULTIES
APPEAL FOR AID TO GOVERNMENT'

(1) Several railway companies many years ago embarked on their own locomotive building.
(2) As the result of an action against the old L.&.N.W. Company they were precluded from building for sale.
(3) Railway companies cannot manufacture for each other.
(4) Railway companies have developed this side of their activity to such an extent that the great locomotive industry of Great Britain which led the world has now to depend almost entirely on its export trade.
(5) Position has become worse since amalgamation by absorption of 18 smaller companies whose engines were ordered from private builders.
(6) In 1919 no fewer than 4,590 locomotives all built by private firms were owned by these concerns, the chief being G.C., N.B. and G.S.W.
(7) Railways are producing up to a third of the total loco producing capacity of the country.
(8) Last year L.M.S. and L.&N.E. placed important orders despite claim that home railways are in a position to manufacture more cheaply than private firms.

(9) There will continue to be diverse opinions on relative cost of two methods of purchase and building.
(10) Railway locomotive designers are in the nature of the case anxious to make experiments under conditions of privacy which are impossible if their work is given out to contract.
(11) Railways may be asked to see whether it is not possible to increase the proportion of support to the home market without curtailing their present engineering activities to a serious degree.

MANCHESTER GUARDIAN – COMMERCIAL
SUPPLEMENT 25th OCTOBER, 1935
ARTICLE ON BRITISH LOCOMOTIVE INDUSTRY
Under the heading
'BRITISH LOCOMOTIVES.
Private Builders' Schemes for More Orders'

EXTRACTS

(1) Predicament of contractors due to increasing tendency in recent years for home railways to undertake the manufacture of their own locomotives, and the great shrinkage in export trade.
(2) Certain railways commenced before the war to build their own locomotives, but there was then a valuable and extensive export market available.
(3) Number of smaller railways before the war purchased all their locomotives; following amalgamation such work was lost to private firms and railway groups have greatly extended their locomotive building activities.
(4) Home orders are now only available under special circumstances such as sudden expansion of traffic.
(5) Private loco builders are deprived of what was before the war the mainstay of their operations.
(6) Loco Manufacturers' Association are asking Government to bring influence to bear on railways to curtail their own building and to put more work outside, loans to be granted for intensive programmes, orders to be placed outside.
(7) Production capacity 1,900 per annum, with estimated employment of 23,000 men – to-day only 9,069 men are employed, in private building shops.
(8) Railway companies are building up to $\frac{1}{3}$rd of the productive capacity of the country.
(9) Competitive capacity of industry in export markets seriously affected by loss of home work.

Internal memo to Sir Harold Hartley from W.V. Wood (Vice President) – 28th October 1935

LOCOMOTIVE INDUSTRY PROPAGANDA

I enclose the cuttings from the 'Yorkshire Post', 18th and 22nd October, and 'Manchester Guardian' of 25th October, to which I referred at the Executive to-day, together with a short summary of the points in each.

Since amalgamation the four railways have built 3,717 locomotives and purchased 1,753 (this, I think, apart from capital additions), and I doubt even for the four groups there has been a decrease in the proportion of locomotive orders given to outside Shops.

I am, however, concerned with the L.M.S. position only. Since amalgamation we have purchased 875 locomotives and built in our own Shops 1,593, and when orders already given are completed in 1936 we shall have purchased 1,065 and built in our own Shops 1,897, the ratio being 36 : 64.

In 1913 I find we purchased 27 and built 126, a ratio of 18 : 82. As further evidence that there has been no change in our policy, the number of purchased locomotives in stock at date of amalgamation was 29.4% and at the end of 1934 30.1%.

You know the reasons which actuated a considerable number of our outside orders, and without stating these or referring to the figures I mention above, I think we should write to each of the locomotive builders who we propose to ask to tender for the new lot of locomotives, asking whether the newspaper statements of the locomotive manufacturers' representations to the Board of Trade are correct, and whether they are parties to them, as the Press statements do not coincide with the facts. I think we should go further and ask to be supplied by the Contractors I mentioned with a copy of the statement to the President of the Board of Trade, informing them that they will be invited to discuss the matter when the document has been considered, as the Company take a very serious view of the misrepresentations which are apparently contained in it.

Letter to Stamp from the Secretary of the Locomotive Manufacturers' Association dated 11th November 1935

Dear Sir

I am informed that several members of my Association received a letter from you on Saturday last in which you deprecate the publication in the 'Yorkshire Post' of 18th October 1935 of an Article relating to the Locomotive Industry.

That Article was not authorised by the Association and its publication had given Members much concern.

On Friday last when meeting Mr Stanier and Mr Gresley with reference to the possibility of establishing a Locomotive Experimental Station, opportunity was taken to mention the matter, and Dr Campbell explained then that we had not been able to trace the source of the Article.

My Committee feel that some explanation is due to you and they have asked me to request that you will see them in London, some time this week if possible, at your convenience. If you would be good enough to state an appointment I would arrange for Members of the Committee to attend.

NOTES OF MEETING WITH THE LOCOMOTIVE MANUFACTURERS ASSOCIATION HELD AT EUSTON, 20th NOVEMBER 1935

PRESENT:

Sir Josiah Stamp
Mr W.V. Wood
Mr E.J.H. Lemon

Representing the Locomotive Manufacturers—

Dr Alec Campbell	Hunslet Engine Co.
Mr F.S. Whalley	Vulcan Foundry
Mr Wm. Lorimer	North British Co.
Mr A.H. Browning	North British Co.
Mr B. Irving	Armstrong Whitworth
Mr E.H.Gregg	Nasmyth Wilson & Co. Ltd
Mr J. W Vaughan	Secretary, Locomotive Manufacturers' Association

Dr Campbell, on behalf of the Association, explained that there were a number of points in connexion with the tenders they were now considering which they would like to discuss.

He explained that they were unable to obtain firm prices for steel, pending a meeting of the Steel trade, which it was thought would not take place until about the 5th December. They were also faced, he stated, with an application for increased wages and restoration of conditions to 1931 standard which might apply to the engineering industry generally from the beginning of January next, and although the locomotive industry was in a much weaker position than the engineering industry generally, there was little doubt that any general increase must apply to locomotive works.

Dr Campbell also explained the difficulty in tendering for work extending for so long a period as 1936/1937, quite apart from the above two unknown factors and he asked that the date for submission of tenders might be extended.

On the question of date, Sir Josiah Stamp explained why he wished to have the figures available before his November Board Meeting, and said that the very latest time and date for that purpose was 2 o'clock on the 27th November. He agreed that these tenders would be regarded as tentative and would be subject to revision in the light of later information by amended tenders to be received by 2 o'clock on the 16th December, explaining that he wished to dispose of the matter, one way or the other, before Christmas.

In answer to questions, Sir Josiah said that the first tenders to be submitted should be on the basis of then known conditions as it was quite possible such tenders would not justify them proceeding further as there was a very narrow margin in justification for this special work. It was not a renewal programme in the ordinary sense, as the engines proposed to be replaced could run for years with their original efficiency. On this point, Sir Josiah emphasised the need for reasonable prices and said it must not be assumed by either the locomotive industry or the steel trade, that an order of this magnitude would be issued in any event. On the other hand, Sir Josiah said if prices were reasonably low there was possibility that the programme might be increased at some date in the future, as we had reduced our original proposal because of the narrow margin.

It was agreed that the builders, in tendering, could put in clauses varying the price in certain contingencies, such as those mentioned, but the measure and amount of such variation must be clear so that on the second tender the railway company's risk would be a definite one and Sir Josiah added he could not contemplate a clause which would merely throw on to the company the whole of the additional liability.

The Association enquired whether there was any special reason for the minimum number of any tender being 25, and they were informed that this was thought to be the lowest economic number possible, and was in accordance with our practice in recent years. It was then suggested that a particular firm might not be able to produce 25 locomotives in two years but could produce 20, and Sir Josiah said while he doubted the possibility of this, he would not shut the door to a smaller number than 25 being tendered for.

A suggestion was then made that the Association might put in one tender, leaving it to the railway company to allocate, and the embarrassment of this to the railway company was explained by reference to difficulties which had arisen in other like cases.

Two of the companies seemed to think that spreading the work over two years added to their risk and it was agreed that if they liked to expedite deliveries to one year and that did not mean loading the price with overtime, etc. the company would have no objection to the expedited work; the two years' spread having been suggested in the interests of the trade.

It was accordingly agreed to proceed on the lines suggested above, and there would be no need for the company to write to each contractor regarding the revised dates, or the tentative nature of the first tender, as the Secretary of the Association will advise each of the companies of the understanding, and each company will in its tender make the agreed reservation regarding the second tender.

After the meeting the Association met in private and subsequently enquired whether the railway company would have any objection to the Steel Casting Association being informed of the nature of the discussion and the need to quote a special firm price, and a reply was sent to the Association that there would be no objection from the railway company's point of view.

No doubt the Chief Mechanical Engineer and Chief Stores Superintendent can make approximate estimates of the variation in prices which would probably be due to:-

(a) conceding the full wages claim
(b) a rise in prices of steel work required, of, say, 5 per cent, 10 per cent, and 15 per cent respectively.

Given the comments in the press, the atmosphere in the meeting must have been interesting and hardly beneficial to an industry about to tender for the largest single order from its biggest customer. The Company duly sent out the tenders to its own timetable and waited for the responses. As would be expected, it then negotiated hard to bring the prices down as described below.

November, 1935, the Trade were asked to tender for:-

227	4–6–0	2-cylinder locomotives and tenders (as above)
69	2–8–0	freight locomotives
73	2–6–4	passenger tank locomotives

in lots of 25, 50, 75, 100, 150, 200 or 227 for the first, 25, 44 or 69 for the second, and 25, 50 or 73 for the third type. As these proposals formed part of the Government loan scheme in addition to ordinary conditions, it was pointed out that all other things being equal, preference would be given to work performed in the Special Areas.

Prior to the date when tenders were to be received, the Locomotive Manufacturers' Association asked for a meeting to discuss a number of points they wished to raise. These included:-

(1) inability to obtain firm prices for steel.
  To meet this point Sir Josiah Stamp, who met the Association, agreed to accept tenders on 27th November, with a reservation on this point, subject to final figures, on 16th December, explaining that the first tenders might not justify the company proceeding further with the orders which were not for ordinary renewal work, as the engines to be replaced could run for years with their original efficiency. He emphasised the need for reasonable prices as the margin in justification for the work was slender, and it must not be assumed that the order

Stanier 2—6—4T Nos. 2602 and 2601 at Crewe North, with their coupling rods not yet refitted, following delivery from North British Locomotive Company in November 1936. Only one lot of these tank engines was built by the trade and the order for 73 locomotives, Nos. 2545-2617, went to North British Locomotive Company although the lowest tender was that of R. Stephenson & Co. North British were £20 higher per locomotive but, owing to their Special Area position in Scotland and the fact that their deliveries would be completed in September 1936 compared with August 1937, they won the order.

COLLECTION R. S. CARPENTER

would be issued in any event. On the other hand, if prices were reasonably low the programme might be increased.

(2) Was there a special reason for the minimum number of 25?
It was explained that this was considered the economic minimum, but smaller lots would be considered.

(3) Would one tender by the Association be acceptable?
This, it was explained, would leave the company with the embarrassment of allocating work, and in other cases had caused difficulty.

227 4–6–0 type	25	50	75	100	150	200	227
	£	£	£	£	£	£	£
Armstrong Whitworth	6,616	6,465	6,350	6,232	6,190	6,161	6,148
North British Loco.	6,515	6,435	6,395	6,275	6,245	6,205	6,195
Vulcan Foundry	6,467	6,386	6,342	6,274	6,226	6,175	6,165
Beyer Peacock	6,650	6,576	6,550	6,500	6,450	6,375	6,360
Others	6,617 to 7,370	6,500 and 6,506	6,446 and 6,475				

The company were later advised by the North British Locomotive Co. Ltd. that their prices, as above, required to be increased by £55 as they had broken some rule of the Association in quoting alternative prices for riveted and welded tanks, the latter at £55 lower had been tendered. The order was, however, settled on above quotations.

The most favourable course for the company was to accept the Armstrong Whitworth offer of—

227 @ £6,148   £1,395,596

The next most favourable course was to accept—

Vulcan Foundry Ltd 75 @ £6,342   £475,650
Armstrong Whitworth 152 @ £6,190   £940,880
                                                        £1,416,530

a course which would have cost the company an extra   £20,934

and given preference to a non special area

It was therefore decided to consider the Armstrong offer only, but as the price of £6,148 was appreciably higher than that paid before or contemplated now, the firm were informed that, while the lowest tender, the company could not place the order at that figure, and they were offered the lot at £6,050. After much discussion of the reasons why prices had advanced so greatly, the figure of £6,080 was mutually agreed, a total reduction of £15,436 on the tender, and the order placed.

69   2–8–0   Goods locomotives and tenders
73   2–6–4   Passenger tank locomotives

The original tenders of the North British Company were the most favourable for each type and each was accepted, but this was withdrawn when that company, as in the case of the 4–6–0 type, withdrew its alternative prices. The position then became:—

2–8–0 type	25	44	69
	£	£	£
Vulcan Foundry	6,580	6,509	6,446
Beyer Peacock	6,655	6,531	6,450
R. Stephenson	6,642	6,500	6,456
North British Loco.	6,614	6,539	6,490
Armstrong Whitworth	6,672	6,566	6,520
W.G. Bagnall	6,693	6,601	6,566
Others	6,628 to 7,200	—	—

The Vulcan offer was then accepted for 69 @ £6,446 ... £444,774

2–6–4 type	25	50	73
	£	£	£
R. Stephenson	5,760	5,626	5,595
North British Loco.	5,735	5,630	5,615
Beyer Peacock	5,750	5,645	5,640
Vulcan Foundry	5,770	5,690	5,670
Armstrong Whitworth	5,780	5,705	5,680
W.G. Bagnall	5,775	5,745	5,725
Others	5,720 to 5,830		

The lowest tender was that of Stephenson & Co. But the tender of the North British Co. £20 more or £1,460 in total, was considered the more acceptable, owing to their position in Scotland and the fact that the deliveries by the North British Company would commence in 18 weeks and at the rate of 3 per week. The whole of the 73 would be delivered in September, 1936. The deliveries by Messrs. Stephenson & Co. would commence by one in the 24th week, and afterwards at the rate of five per month, the deliveries would not be completed until August, 1937.

The tendered prices for each of the three types are subject to an addition in any general increases in the basic rates of wages after June, 1936, is made, such addition being only in respect of outstanding work at that date. As this condition applied to all the tendered prices the price comparisons as between the different firms are unaffected.

Not surprisingly the unsuccessful bidders were unhappy with their failure to take a share in these massive orders as shown in a memo to Stamp from W.V. Wood on 6th January 1936:-

ORDERS FOR NEW LOCOMOTIVES

Mr Bruce Gardner [of Armstrong Whitworth] telephoned me to-day and told me that he was having further difficulty with the Vulcan Foundry Company regarding the order given to the Armstrong Whitworth Company.

There was considerable difficulty last month when it became known that Armstrong Whitworth had reduced their price below that tendered, and Mr Gardner explained to all the members of the Locomotive Manufacturers' Association that:—

1. His Company's tender for the locomotives ordered from them was the lowest in any event, and, therefore, the Trade were not prejudiced by the further reduction agreed.

2. He was informed by the railway company that while his company's tender was the lowest, it appreciably exceeded the figure included in their estimate when submitting the scheme to the Treasury and that the company could not place the order at the tender figure.

3. The matter was discussed at considerable length with the company and it emerged they were under no obligation or necessity to purchase these locomotives at this time, and would only do so at a price which they thought reasonable.

The company's estimated cost of construction, together with what they regarded as an adequate allowance for profit, and allowance for rise in prices was mentioned, and eventually the reduced figure was agreed between the parties.

Mr Bruce Gardner asked me whether I was in general agreement with him, as he understood that Mr Whalley [of Vulcan Foundry] refused to accept the position and stated that it was untrue. I said he had stated the position correctly but that I would add a fourth point:-

4. This particular block of locomotives represents a premature replacement of locomotives in serviceable condition and not locomotives requiring renewal in the ordinary course. Apart, therefore, from construction cost considerations, there was a point beyond which it would not pay the company to build these locomotives as it would be cheaper to continue using the old units for years to come, with, perhaps, a few exceptions which could be ignored.

Meanwhile there was the question of the Company's response to the Locomotive Manufacturers' Association submission to the Board of Trade. The 'spinning' from the Trade continued as the LMS waited for the Association to respond to its comments:-

30th January 1936 Memo from W. V. Wood to The Chairman

LOCOMOTIVE MANUFACTURERS' ASSOCIATION
With reference to Mr Vaughan's letter of the 27th January, I think you might reply to the effect that your letter of the 24th January did not make a definite time limit of a week but suggested a period of within, say, a week, and that you would like to know approximately when the comments of the Association will be received, as a day or two over a week is neither here nor there, but if the comments are unlikely to be received within a reasonably short time you must reconsider procedure, adding, that in the meantime you will defer sending your comments to the Board of Trade.

As regards the last sentence of Mr Vaughan's letter, I suggest the Association should be asked to submit, in writing, the points they wish to raise (as you have done in your memorandum) and it will then be considered whether the meeting is necessary and if so, with you.

I attach an extract from the 'Financial Times' of the 27th January, with some comments which Mr Clifton has made upon it. At first I thought we should refer to this in relation to this matter, but the Association could of course say that the article did not originate from them although its context would appear to imply that it did. I therefore think that we might keep the matter in cold storage and raise it if necessary if there is a meeting with the Association.

'RAILWAY EQUIPMENT MAKERS' SCOPE FOR INCREASED EARNINGS'
Financial Times – 27th January 1936

1) 'The companies supplying equipment to the railways have passed through a very bad time since the war, and in the pre-depression period they were already being affected by the railway companies' policy of supplying more and more of their own requirements.'

This point has been dealt with in paragraphs (7) and (8) of our memorandum on the Locomotive Manufacturers' Association 'case', where it is shewn that only in the depression period have the railway orders shown a decline.

2) 'It is a condition of the schemes (£26,500,000 Guarantee) that the railways shall not use the loans to finance operations in their own shops, but shall place orders with outside companies.'

There is no such restrictive condition. The Act provides for 'preference being given, other things being equal, to firms in the Special Areas'. In fact it is further provided that if any work is carried out by any of the railway companies by direct labour, the wages and other conditions of employment shall be those in force in the company's service on similar work.

The arrangement with regard to the Special Areas of course affects the placing of orders with outside firms where that is done.

3) 'British manufacturers have suffered since the post-war grouping of the railway companies.'

This was one point contained in the Locomotive Manufacturers' Association 'case' and it was refuted in paragraph (7) of our memorandum.

4) 'Relations between British locomotive makers and the British railways are still important, though not much business has passed.'

The point is answered in paragraphs (7) and (19) in our memorandum dealing with the Locomotive Manufacturers' Association 'case'.

5) 'A glance at the table will show that the carriage-manufacturing companies have returned much more stable profits than manufacturers of locomotives. Their stability is due partly to the larger purchasing by the railways.'

This infers railway companies should provide manufacturers' profits at the expense of transport. The matter has been dealt with in paragraph (16) of our memorandum dealing with the Locomotive Manufacturers' Association 'case'.

Letter from Stamp to J. W. Vaughan, Locomotive Manufacturers' Association 5th February 1936

Dear Sir
I am in receipt of your letter of the 27th ultimo. In my letter to you of the 24th January I suggested a period of within, say, a week, and I shall be glad if you will let me know approximately when I may expect to receive the comments of your Association, as if they are unlikely to reach me within a reasonably short time, I shall have to reconsider procedure.

In the meantime I will defer sending forward to the Board of Trade our comments on the memorandum submitted by your Association.

With regard to the last sentence of your letter, I shall be glad if you will, in the first place, submit in writing the points which your Committee desire to raise.

Letter from J. W. Vaughan LMA to Stamp, 6th February 1936

Dear Sir Josiah Stamp
In reply to your letter of yesterday's date and with further reference to your letter of 24th January last I have been in communication with Members of the Association but I find that it is impossible to call Members together at a reasonably early date to consider and discuss your commentary upon the Memorandum which this Association submitted to the Board of Trade in October last.

In the circumstances I do not feel justified in suggesting that you should any longer delay forwarding your commentary to the Board of Trade.

I am directed to thank you for your courtesy in letting us see in advance a copy of that commentary.

Stamp to the President of the Board of Trade 7th February 1936

My dear President,
In the course of recent discussions with the locomotive trade arising out of orders we were placing with them for locomotives, I told them that I was extremely surprised at the statements which had appeared in the press which claimed to be based upon representations made to you by the Locomotive Manufacturers' Association in regard to the relationship between the trade and the railway companies.

I was informed that they are not responsible for the press statements and the Association sent me a copy of the actual representations made to you on 9th October last. After reading these I decided that I would forward to you this company's comments on these representations, and on the 24th January, I sent a draft to the Locomotive Manufacturers' Association so that they could make any comments they wished upon my draft before submission to you.

I have been informed by the Locomotive Manufacturers' Association that it is impossible to call their members together at a reasonably early date to consider and discuss my comments, and therefore they do not feel justified in suggesting that they should be delayed any longer.

I accordingly enclose a copy of the memorandum I have prepared on the subject, which I have of course confined to the questions raised insofar as they affect the railway companies and particularly my own company.

Yours very truly, Chairman

LMS MEMORANDUM TO THE BOARD OF TRADE

(1) In October last the Press contained references to representations by the Locomotive Manufacturers' Association to the Government in regard to the manufacture of locomotives from which it could only be inferred that either the President of the Board of Trade or the Press has been misinformed. Each locomotive builder who had received orders from this company was therefore asked for a copy of the actual representations and this was received while the company were discussing orders upon the trade for new locomotives. These orders have now been issued and the following comments in the Locomotive Manufacturers' representations are made on behalf of the L.M.S. Company, a copy having been supplied to the Locomotive Manufacturers' Association.

(2) The representations referred to are the case submitted to the President of the Board of Trade on 9th October 1935. Where this deals with matters not affecting the British railways no comments are necessary, and owing to the fact that the L.M.S. Company is only once referred to directly it is necessary for this memorandum to deal with references to the four amalgamated companies.

(3) The Association have not correctly described the facts relating to the construction of locomotives by the British railways. It dates back to at least 1845, and whatever may have actuated the early construction work for many years prior to the outbreak of War in 1914 it was not, as suggested in the Locomotive Manufacturers' 'case', an 'adjunct' to railway repair shops but an integral function of railway locomotive shops for reasons of economy.

(4) It is hardly necessary to explain the use made by the Government of the railway companies workshops during the War, and the position which arose after 1918 when the railway equipment, which, owing to precedence of purely War work, required complete overhaul.

(5) On the termination of Government possession of the railways in August 1921, the task of physical reconditioning was only beginning and the companies were at the same time faced with the re-organizations and re-arrangements required by the grouping legislation of the Government.

(6) In this re-organization which took several years to effect so far as it related to its workshops, the L.M.S. Company proceeded on a planned scheme of rationalization. This was based on its rolling stock production requirements – whether complete units, parts or repairs – and involved facing the problems of capital re-arrangements, modernization of appliances, layout of processes and changed employment of staff. As part of this scheme, the previous locomotive building work at Horwich, Stoke, Barrow, St. Rollox (Glasgow), Kilmarnock and Inverness was discontinued and all such work concentrated at Crewe and Derby. The output of locomotives at these two shops was planned for normal production in co-ordination with other work, below the previous output of new locomotives in the company's shops, but with capacity to increase output if required, thus leaving a substantial margin for outside orders to be given to the trade.

(7) It is therefore completely inaccurate to suggest that the company has since 1913, or since the War, altered its policy in a manner which caused a diversion of its requirements from the locomotive manufacturing trade. It has so far adhered to the policy mentioned above; that is indicated by the facts that on amalgamation the proportion of the company's locomotive stock which represented complete units built by the trade was 29 ⅓rd per cent (3,029 out of a total stock of 10,316), and of the orders since then (and prior to the memorandum submitted by the Association to the Government) 36 per cent (1,065 out of a total of 2,962) were placed with the trade.

(8) Reverting to the position as it affects the British railway companies as a whole, the statement of the Association is also inaccurate, and the further statement that the British railways now produce practically all their own locomotives is grossly inaccurate. In the twelve years 1923/1934 the published returns of locomotives renewed by the four companies shew that they built 3,717 and purchased 1,753, or in the ratio 68 to 32 compared with 366 and 46 respectively, in the ratio 89 to 11, in 1913. It may be added that it was only in the years 1931 to 1933 which were 'occasions of emergency' to the railway companies that locomotives supplied by the trade fell below 100.

(9) Turning to the economy of construction in the railway companies' shops it is alleged that:–
  (a) The manufacturer is more likely to carry out his work economically than the one who manufactures as a side line.
  (b) The railway companies are building, without competition.
  (c) Co-operation between the manufacturers and the railway companies is almost entirely lacking.
  (d) The railway companies have made vague objections to the claims of the manufacturers.
  (e) These objections always centre on the claim, never substantiated, that the railways can manufacture more cheaply than they can purchase from the trade.
  (f) This claim has never been supported by quotation of definite figures or details such as were desired by the manufacturers for the purpose of close examination and comparison of respective costs which they have thought so desirable. The only comparisons have taken the form of percentages indicating an advantage of 40 to 50 per cent which no one could accept seriously.
  (g) Where construction and repairs are not segregated efficiency is weakened and costs are uneconomic.

(10) These statements are all connected as parts of a suggestion of wasteful work which is categorically denied.

(11) Railway construction work is not a side line but part of a comprehensive use of equipment and plant for the co-ordinated manufacture of parts used in repairs, partial renewals of stock in service and in the construction of new boilers and new locomotives. The economic advantage of this combination is marked and is due mainly to the regulation of the flow of work, which, in its parts varies during the times of the year, with regular employment of the staff and equipment. In part it is almost due to the fact that it is the equipment and layout of the shops are kept up to the most modern requirements and practices; the use of plant which is out of date or uneconomical is discontinued and redundant plant is scrapped and written off. Against this, railway shop costs are higher because of higher rates of wages and the fact that they have not the advantage of de-rating to manufacturers, other than railway companies.

(12) There is true competition between the L.M.S. Railway shops' and manufacturers' selling prices for all requirements which can either be purchased or manufactured. Where purchase appears to be cheaper, manufacture is discontinued, the plant being retained in some cases against an undue rise in prices. Similarly, where prices have risen unduly for articles previously purchased, manufacture by the company has resulted in substantial savings. In the reverse case, where purchase prices are higher than railway shop costs and, for the reasons mentioned in paras (6) and (7) the company do not cater for their whole requirements, it is recognized that manufacturers' costs are affected adversely by the economy of the company's shop arrangements and allowance is made for this in placing orders, and only when the gap is too large is such work withdrawn from manufacturers or selling agencies and transferred to the company's shops. Recently it would appear that various trade associations have made arrangements under which selling prices are inflated by additions to compensate the non-successful tenderers. The foregoing indicates that the general policy of the company and the effect of its application to locomotive orders has, as already seen (para (7)) resulted in a greater proportion of orders for new locomotives being placed with the trade. Only in two cases has it been ultimately necessary to place a contemplated order on the locomotive trade in the company's shops, and costs in those cases were specifically examined after completion of the work, and the transfers were found to have been justified.

(13) Exactly what is envisaged by the reference to the alleged lack of co-operation, and where this has been suggested to or discouraged by the railway companies, is not stated but it is not assisted by misstatements on the part of the trade, in the 'case' and elsewhere, of the facts in relation to the railways. The only suggestion of co-operation which can be traced, apart from those in the form of railway companies' orders and recent proposals of the railway companies in regard to a Testing Station, arose out of a motion in the House of Lords by Lord Dudley in April 1933, when the Government spokesman suggested that the parties should discuss rationalization together. Following this, the railway companies informed the Government in reply to their enquiry that they were prepared to discuss the question if the manufacturers desired.

(14) Whenever it has been suggested by a contractor or associations that the company's costs were in any way unsound, this has been met by an offer from the company of a mutual exchange and examination of detailed costs. No trace of any such suggestion to the L.M.S. Company in respect of locomotives can be traced. On the only occasions where such offers to other trades were accepted, the contractors concerned agreed the facts and withdrew allegations similar to those now made. On the occasions when L.M.S. rolling stock costs have been examined by manufacturers, the latter have eventually suggested that they are prejudiced because railway costs are lower than those of manufacturers, owing to the coordination of repair and construction work in railway shops, with the resultant spread of work and overheads.

(15) While there is no desire to intervene in any way in regard to the questions of export trade, the company considers that in certain respects, apart from those mentioned above, the 'case' in reference to both export and home orders is incomplete or inexact.

(16) The world-wide reduction in the need for steam locomotives arising out of the development of other forms of rail traction and road traction has been accentuated by the greater use now being obtained per locomotive with the consequent reductions in stock requirements.

Class 5 No. 5398, pictured at Crewe in September 1937, was built by Armstrong Whitworth as part of the largest single order placed by a British railway company with an outside manufacturer. The order for 227 engines and tenders was valued at £1.38 million. The LMS had requested prices for batches of 25, 50, 75, 100, 150, 200 and 227, and Armstrong Whitworth were not the cheapest quote until the number reached 75. Above that there was little to choose between Armstrong Whitworth, North British Locomotive Company and Vulcan Foundry, but after negotiation, Armstrong Whitworth won the total order, albeit at £98 each below their original tender, with North British losing out partly because of a technical error in their bid and Vulcan Foundry because they were not in a Special Area. COLLECTION JOHN JENNISON

(The L.M.S. stock, for example, has fallen from 10,444 in 1923 to 7,915 including 430 stored in a serviceable condition at December 1935). This has necessarily contrasted the demands for new locomotives. The failure in the 'case' to provide proper background in a recognition of this heavy fall in the total *absolute* requirements of the railways makes all the comparative or relative statements misleading or tendentious. Moreover this contraction of demand appears from the Locomotive Manufacturers' 'case' to have been accompanied by an actual expansion of the *capacity* of the industry. In considering the National aspect of the question it is clearly desirable to bear in mind the National importance of economy in transport. The effect of the suggestion in the Locomotive Manufacturers' 'case' that the railway companies should curtail their building work would clearly increase railway costs, and therefore re-act on transport costs borne by industry in general.

(17) In this connexion it may be noted that roughly 42 per cent of the outlay on a new locomotive in the L.M.S. shops represents materials for fabrication purchased from various British sources, and not only would the proposal alter the course of trade in this direction but there would be appreciable further reductions in railway employment in Crewe and Derby with its labour and housing re-actions.

(18) The table shown in the 'case' would be more valuable if it were expanded to shew the volume of *all* business of the trade and division of this between home and overseas business, together with insertion of all the years since 1920. This would then indicate the relative changes in the volume of home and export work since 1913.

(19) Reference is made in the Locomotive Manufacturers' 'case' to important orders placed in 1934 by the L.&N.E. and L.M.S. Companies. The L.M.S. orders on the trade between 1923 and 1933 totalled 915 locomotives, and their orders of 150 in 1934 bringing

the total to 1934 to 1,065 were in continuance of their policy throughout. The further lot of 369 locomotives ordered from the trade in December 1935, was also in continuance of that policy. These locomotives were specially financed by means of the Government Loan Scheme, and this particular proposal was submitted to the Chancellor of the Exchequer on 2nd August 1935, it being explained at the time that 'subject to satisfactory prices it would be possible to place at least four-fifths of the work with the locomotive building industry which is suffering severely from lack of overseas orders at the present time'. For reasons which arose since July the programme was reduced by about one-fifth, and 100 per cent of the adjusted programme was, in fact, placed with the locomotive building trade.

(20) In conclusion, it is submitted by the company that the facts as explained above completely disprove the suggestion that the amalgamation of the railways has contributed to the difficulties of the locomotive building trade, and shew to be without foundation the statement that the British railways now produce nearly all their own locomotives, and so far as the L.M.S. is concerned, the policy adopted by it, not only generally, but in connexion with the recent loan scheme, has been one of endeavouring to assist the trade so far as was in its power to do so, notwithstanding the very great difficulties which the company itself has had to contend with in recent years.

As a post-script, it is interesting to compare the overall locomotive purchases for the four companies during the final decade before World War 2, after which the LMS made only one further order from the Trade.

MAIN LINE RAILWAYS
AMOUNT SPENT ON LOCOMOTIVES BUILT OR PURCHASED –
AS PER PUBLISHED ACCOUNTS

	GWR			LNER		
Year	In Company Shops	By Contractors		In Company Shops	By Contractors	
1913	144,563	1,552	146,115	389,386	60,360	449,746
1929	427,326	172,396	599,722	361,164	87,717	448,881
1930	335,990	362,814	698,804	282,323	30,876	313,199
1931	388,905	205,211	594,116	191,344	147,314	338,658
1932	261,465		261,465	137,974	1,720	139,694
1933	277,432		277,432	3,111		3,111
1934	283,179		283,179	217,080	97,093	314,173
1935	378,360		378,360	333,319	127,442	460,761
1936	426,043	6,826	432,869	348,114	174,173	522,287
1937	473,215		473,215	317,067	202,569	519,636
1938	490,588		490,588	464,109		464,109
1929–38	3,742,503	747,247	4,489,750	2,655,605	868,904	3,524,509

	LMS			TOTAL★		
Year	In Company Shops	By Contractors		In Company Shops	By Contractors	
1913	261,711	85,394	347,105	857,358	147,306	1,004,664
1929	840,262	142,176	982,438	1,732,922	402,289	2,135,211
1930	662,540	297,822	960,362	1,391,500	691,512	2,083,012
1931	459,491	363	459,854	1,152,759	352,888	1,505,647
1932	427,596	8,601	436,197	901,763	10,321	912,084
1933	607,765	3,173	610,938	929,996	3,173	933,169
1934	668,845	497,991	1,166,836	1,223,977	595,084	1,819,061
1935	784,632	869,775	1,654,107	1,556,991	997,217	2,554,208
1936	565,598	1,362,107	1,927,705	1,364,083	1,543,106	2,907,109
1937	245,624	772,484	1,018,108	1,076,990	975,053	2,052,043
1938	492,311	493	492,804	1,478,702	493	1,479,195
1929–38	5,754,664	3,954,985	9,709,649	12,809,683	5,571,136	18,380,819

All figures from 1929–1938 are for expenditure on Renewals account – except for the LMS the expenditure on Capital account was insignificant. In 1937 it spent £359,660 and in 1938 £77,687 on capital account, of which £256,252 was purchased externally.

★ The Southern Railway did not buy from the trade during this period

In the ten years from 1929 to 1938 the LMS had purchased 42% of its new locomotives by value from the Trade compared with 25% for the LNER, 17% for the GWR and none for the Southern. Its purchases during the four years 1933–37 totalled over £3.75 million and were for four classes of locomotive:–

Builder	Total	2–6–4T	Class 5	Jubilee	8F
Vulcan Foundry	169		100		69
North British Loco.	173	73		50	50
Armstrong Whitworth	327		327		
	669	73	427	50	119

The final purchase from the trade came during the second World War, for a batch of 2–8–0s which was originally planned for construction at Crewe.

50 2–8–0 Locos. constructed for L.M.S by N.B. Loco. Co. Ltd. under Ministry of Supply Contract.

In July 1941 the L.M.S. asked the N.B. Loco. Co. to quote for the building of 50 2–8–0 locos with six-wheeled tenders. The price quoted by the firm was £12,650 net delivered f.o.r. their works, Glasgow. As an alternative the firm stated it would be willing to consider a proposal to regard the contract as if it were an extension of one upon which they were engaged for the Ministry of Supply.

The L.M.S. considered the quotation of £12,650 to be very high in view of their own costs, and it was agreed with the N.B. Loco. Co. that there should be a mutual exchange of prices. (Information exchanged between the two companies was to be treated in confidence.) After examination the L.M.S. representatives reported that the comparative construction costs excluding interest on capital and/or profit) were L.M.S. £9,102 and N.B.L. £10,723, the difference in L.M.S. favour being due to:–

	£
Lower wages cost due to improved layout and plant	393
Lower manufacturing and purchase price of materials	457
Lower oncost probably due to improved layout and plant	771
	1,621

After completion of the massive orders in the late-1930s, new locomotive construction on the LMS slowed considerably and was all done in the Company's shops except for one final purchase from the trade in 1941/42. 2–8–0 No. 8180 pictured at Elstree in May 1948 was one of fifty built by North British Locomotive Company in an order diverted from Crewe Works because of the wartime production constraints there. As with all their locomotive buying, the LMS drove a hard bargain and secured the engines and tenders for £10,715 each compared with North British Locomotive Company's original quote of £12,650. COLLECTION JOHN JENNISON

Assuming a profit addition of 7% the L.M.S. representatives considered N.B. Co's. quotation should have been £11,500, a reduction of £1,150 on their quotation.

The outcome of the examination was that a contract was placed with the firm for 50 locos as part of the M.of S. Contract, the terms being:–

(a) Maximum price of £11,500 each, including profit
(b) Final price to depend upon actual cost plus profit with the limit given in (a) above.
(c) Maximum price of £11,500 to be adjusted in respect of
  (1) Different details incorporated in M.O.S. contract
  (2) Profit of £700 per loco, to be allowed.

The L.M.S Co. supplied a considerable quantity of material for this contract and the firm were charged cost price, including overheads and carriage, but not interest or profit. The final cost as investigated and certified by the M.O.S. was £10,715.10.0d each made up of:–

	£.s.d.
Materials	5,018.11.2
Direct Labour	3,012.4.10
Overheads at 65% on direct labour	1,957.19.2
Profit	700.0.0
	10,688.15.2
Loco. Manufacturers Association levy at % on selling price	26.14.10
	£10,715.10.0

Once again the Company had brought its supplier to heel.

FURTHER INFORMATION ON
LMS LOCOMOTIVE PROFILES

From the series editor, DAVID HUNT

Once more I am delighted to be able to make some of the comments and additions sent in by readers of our works available for wider dissemination. It is always a pleasure to receive such information and comment and I thank all those who have contributed. Our own researches are also ongoing and continue to bear fruit so I am glad to have the almost unique opportunity of being able to write this column to supplement our books in order to bring as many people as possible up to date with what we are finding out.

General

Several readers have queried why the Vulcan Foundry allocated what were called 'Rogation Numbers' to engines built there instead of the more familiar Works Numbers. It does seem a strange word to use and is usually associated with the three days before Ascension Day in the Christian calendar but it can also be taken to mean supplication, petition, appeal, request or application. I would imagine, therefore, that it was in the sense of request or application, i.e., a request from a customer for an engine to be built and hence akin to order number. Why it should have been used in preference to more mundane terms, though, I can't state.

Pictorial Supplement to LMS Locomotive Profile No. 5 – The Mixed traffic Class 5s No. 5000–5224

There is a mistake in the caption on page 66 – No. 45084 had a vertical throatplate boiler when it was photographed in May 1954.

LMS Locomotive Profile No. 9 – The Main-Line Diesel-Electrics

I have been told that in a recent article in another publication it was stated that Nos. 10000 and 10001 were not allowed to operate in multiple for about ten years after entering service and that until the late 1950s they were simply working in tandem when coupled together, with drivers in each locomotive controlling them independently. I have looked into this and am grateful for help from Adrian Ford, who

worked on the locomotives from 1956 before becoming Senior Electrical Inspector Locomotives (Testing) at Derby and knew men who were involved with them from the beginning. None of the men we have spoken to who worked as fitters, mechanical and electrical inspectors or drivers on the locomotives has any recollection of any such ban and we have been unable to find any primary documentary evidence for it. The only problem recalled by drivers was that before the inner portions of the front body fairings were removed from 10000 in May 1949, it was an awkward job to connect the jumper cables for multiple working. Adrian also tells me that the maintenance schedule for the locomotives called for functional tests of the multiple working features, for which a test set was produced when they were built, and the tests were definitely carried out on a regular basis.

When working in multiple, the locomotives were generally coupled with the No. 2 ends together. This was because of the unreliability of the train-heating boilers, which led to an extra man being carried to monitor and operate them and it therefore made sense for them to be adjacent to each other. It is possible, therefore, that the presence of a man in the leading cab of the second locomotive has been assumed to indicate that there was another driver.

Some other erroneous statements have been made recently in other publications about the 'twins', such as them being air braked, whereas in reality both were only vacuum fitted, and the clean air compartments being adjacent to the No. 2 cabs, which was actually the location of the train-heating boiler compartments.

When describing the operation of water scoops fitted for topping-up the boiler tanks, I omitted in the *Profile* to state that only 10000 had the rather inconvenient system whereby the fireman had to leave the cab when approaching a trough and operate the scoop from the boiler compartment in accordance with light indications from the driver. No. 10001 had the much more logical arrangement in which the scoop could be operated from the cab.

LMS Locomotive Profile No. 11 – The 'Coronation' Class Pacifics

Tom Robertson, who on his own admission used to 'bunk' Polmadie shed frequently in his youth, tells me that the photograph of 46227 on page 39 was not taken there but was, in his words, 'about as far as a Polmadie engine could go – it's Camden.' My apologies for that. All I offer as an excuse is that 'Polmadie' is written on the back of the print and since my misspent youth was at Edge Hill, I ask to be forgiven.

Thanks to Ian Townend, we have looked more closely at when 6231 received 1946-style lined black livery. There is a photograph of the engine with smoke deflectors and coupled to a de-streamlined Mk 4 tender but still wearing unlined black livery with scroll-and-serif cabside numbers and tender lettering in the high position. Since the addition of smoke deflectors and de-streamlining of the tender are documented in history cards, it would appear that the 1946 livery wasn't applied until May 1947 when the engine left Crewe Works on the 30th of the month following a light service repair. The cabside numbers, however, were plain without the inset lining that first appeared on 6230 in September 1946, although the tender lettering had the lining.

Also from Ian comes photographic confirmation that 6236 had its front cab windows enlarged prior to late May / early June 1952. This means that the only likely time for its alteration was during a Heavy General repair ending on 30th November 1951, which date should therefore be included in Appendix C on page 167.

Another piece of Ian's detective work concerns the restoration of 6247's smokebox to cylindrical form. From analysis of photographs he has determined that this happened while 6220 still had a sloping smokebox and the carriages of the Royal Scot were still carmine and cream. Hence, the alteration must have been made before the summer of 1956 and was more than likely during a Heavy Intermediate repair ending on 21st May 1955. The date given in Appendix C should therefore be amended.

Ian Townend has also added to our list of locomotives with nameplates having red backgrounds, all being in green livery with early BR emblems. No. 6228 was seen with them in July 1957, No. 6236 on 21st August 1957, No. 6247 still with a sloping smokebox probably in 1954 or 1955, and 6248, again with a sloping smokebox, in June 1955. There is also an addition to the list of tenders with incorrect right-facing BR crests, 6243 being seen with one when in green livery and with a sloping smokebox.

Pictorial Supplement to LMS Locomotive Profile No. 11 – The 'Coronation' Class Pacifics

The caption to the photograph of No. 6233 on page 49 incorrectly states that it was the last 'Coronation' to wear LMS red livery. As correctly stated elsewhere in both the *Profile* and *Supplement*, this distinction rests with 6232.

We couldn't date the photograph on the rear cover when the Supplement was prepared, but Ian Townend has identified it as being taken by Douglas Docherty on 25th July 1959. No. 6220 was at the head of the 10.05 am Birmingham 'Scotsman' and the 'Royal Scot' in the distance was being hauled by 6221.

LMS Locomotive Profile No. 12 – The Diesel-Electric Shunters

Graham Smith wrote to point out that having mentioned the later Dutch and Australian versions of the LMS/EE twin-motor locomotives, we omitted any reference to those made for ICI at Dick, Kerr Works. There were seven of them, three built in 1948 and four in 1951, two of which have been preserved – EE works number 1553 built in 1948 and currently masquerading as 12139 at the North York Moors Railway, and works number 1901 built in 1951 and presently at Llangollen.

Graham also referred to No. 15107 built at Swindon for the Western Region of BR in 1949, which we failed to mention even though it was closely similar to the Brush-built LNER 15004 that we did discuss. There were similar Brush locomotives built for the CIE, industrial users and Nigeria, as well as some built in Australia, but we left them out as well. All I can state is that having set out to describe those locomotives used by the LMS and by BR to an LMS/EE design, we had to draw the line somewhere in our coverage. For readers who want to find out more, *Brush Diesel locomotives 1940–1978* by George Toms published by Turntable Publications & The Transport Publishing Co., 1978 has many details.

Graham's last point is that there are some splendid views of one of the Derby-built WD locomotives, possibly 878, in the old film *The Great St. Trinian's Train Robbery*.

LMS Locomotive Profile No. 13 – The Standard Compounds

Stephen Lea doubts that when the photograph of 1004 on page 48 was taken at Leicester, the engine was in charge of the 9.30 am Scotch express from St. Pancras as stated in the caption. As he points out, the carriages behind the tender consist of a close-coupled set of six-wheelers dating from 1882–1883 and it is unlikely that such vehicles would have been part of a Scotch express in 1909. Furthermore, a close examination shows that the engine was not buffered up to the carriages and was standing on the middle road fully coaled. A more likely explanation is that No. 1004, which at the time was a Holbeck engine, was waiting for the express to arrive, when it would take it on to Leeds.

The gremlins crept into the table of Variations as Built at Appendix C. On page 163 the date for the alterations including left-hand drive beginning with No. 1085 should be May 1925, whilst that for differences introduced on 1185 *et seq* should be February 1927 and not as shown.

LMS Locomotive Profile No. 14 – The Standard Class 3 Goods Tank Engines

Jim Perkins, who worked at Nottingham shed, sent the following informative and interesting comment on the photograph of No. 7109 on page ii:

'The picture shows the engine just leaving the shed to go out on target No 1, which by 1965 was a spare local trip category, and looking at the bunker it had probably just been topped up with water and coal. The viewpoint is from the 1868 coaling stage banking looking across to Middle Furlong Road, the houses of which can be seen in the background. The area between the lines in the foreground, which led to the 1868 built No.1 shed, and the road behind the sleeper fence was known as the 'Field Side' because that is what it was when the shed was built – an area of fields and crocus meadows in which the nearly extinct Nottingham crocus grew. The road names from the point where the photographer stood were (7) Coalstage, (6) Ashpit, (4 & 5) Independent, (3) Stack Side (coal stacks), (2) Mid Stack (coal stacks) and (1) Field Side. Furlong/ Peyton House now stands where Field Side and the coal stacks once stood, while Middle Furlong Road has been largely obliterated to be replaced by a new road. Only a very short section next to W. Furse still exists and the only remnant of the shed site is a short stretch of the boundary wall.

'The NE wagon contained two sets of wheels that were probably destined for a job under the shear legs in No. 1 shed (this was a few years before the drop pit was installed), which was used for freight engines.

'As an apprentice at 16A (1959–1964) I only occasionally worked on the two Jockos then based at Nottingham and had more to do with the Diesel Jockos than the 0–6–0Ts. Even doing running repairs on shed we rarely saw them as they were out in either Nottingham or Beeston Yards. They were in fact just two representatives lost in our legions of 8Fs, 4Fs and 2Ps and by 1961 our sole example was 47631. That nine survived the gas axe is a miracle.'

John Miles has contacted us to say that the caption on page 61 to the picture showing two push-pull engines is incorrect in stating that the location is Clydach on the Abergavenny – Merthyr line and that it is actually Clydach-on-Tawe. Thus, the suggestion that they were possibly on loan to Tredegar or Abergavenny is also incorrect, as is the comment on page 54. Unfortunately, we cannot identify every location and depend in many instances on the information that comes with the photograph, but at least the request for any reader who can help to come forward has enabled us to set the record straight.

We welcome any feedback from readers, especially amendments or additions that can be disseminated via David Hunt's Further Information column that appears from time to time in this publication. We also welcome queries and will always try to help wherever we can, but in order to help us out we would ask that David, as series editor, is the first point of contact for any communication regarding the series. If John Jennison or I receive any reader input, it almost invariably ends up on David's doormat, so to save time it is best if it goes to him in the first place. Therefore, please send any emails to *davehunt@madasafish.com* or letters via Wild Swan Publications.   Editor

We regret that *LMS Locomotive Profiles* Nos. 1, 2 and 3 are now out of print.

The Shaftsbury Collection

Cty. Taunton Model Railway Group

Regular *LMS Journal* contributor Graham Warburton submitted these five pictures, and another of the LMSJ team, John Edgington, wrote the captions. They were taken by Geoff Lumb and are part of the Shaftsbury collection that was purchased by two members of the Taunton Model Railway Group some years ago. As editor I welcome contributions of this nature and would like to take the opportunity to say that I am always pleased to be offered pictures, either single views or a themed set, for publication. They need not be captioned as this can be arranged, and my preference is for LMS period views or early British Railways period.

LNWR 'Special Tank' No. 7276 with empty stock at Euston station platform 4. When the picture was taken, the locomotive was not coupled to the stock and was carrying a locomotive headlamp at both ends of the locomotive. No. 7276 was built as LNWR No. 1262 at Crewe in October 1862, eventually to become LMS 7276 in July 1926 before being withdrawn in December 1930.

LMS Jubilee 4–6–0 No. 5554 entering Platform 3 at Euston during the late summer of 1934. The locomotive was new in June 1934 and is seen carrying an enamel shed plate, replaced by cast-iron in January 1935. No. 5554 was named Ontario on 11th March 1936. The tender, a Fowler 3500 gallon pattern, was later to be replaced with a Stanier 4000 gallon type. The engine was withdrawn in November 1964.

LNWR 4–4–2T 'Precursor Tank' built at Crewe as LNWR No. 196 and renumbered 6793 by the LMS in August 1927, being withdrawn in December 1931. The location was Euston station platform 3, and the loco was probably on empty stock workings although it was not coupled to the coaches and the engine is seen with both head and tail lamps.

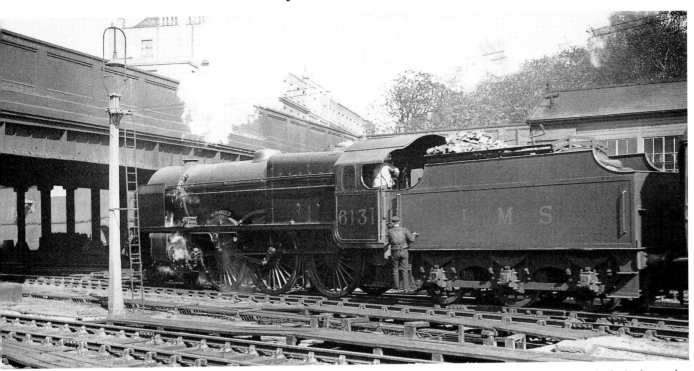

LMS 'Royal Scot' class 4—6—0 No. 6131 Planet *prior to departing from platform 12 at Euston, with Euston No. 2 signal box in the background. The likely date is late summer 1934. The locomotive was renamed* The Royal Warwickshire Regiment *on 26th March 1936. No. 6131 was built by the North British Locomotive Company, Glasgow, in 1927 and rebuilt with a tapered boiler in October 1944, being withdrawn in October 1962. The Fowler 3500 gallon tender seen here was later replaced with a Stanier 4000 gallon type. The man standing on the footstep appears to be a shunter who may have been giving the driver some last-minute information.*

LMS Fowler 2—6—4T No. 2375 banking a train out of platform 12 at Euston, most likely the one hauled by 6131 (in the previous photograph). No. 2375 was built at Derby in 1932 and withdrawn in 1962. The coach, 57ft composite 1st/3rd 3510, was built at Wolverton in 1924 to Diagram D1694.

Enginemen's Record Cards

by BOB ESSERY

Recently Robin Cullup showed me several examples of small cards and asked if they were of interest. They were. I had never seen enginemen's record cards quite like them before, and enquiries with other ex-railwaymen produced no positive answer, so I felt that maybe some reader might be able to help.

The cards measure 150mm x 120mm and the reference in the top right-hand corner is $\text{P.F.}\frac{1189}{2/25}$ which, together with the way L.M.&S.R. has been written suggests this is an early LMS period adaption of a pregroup company document that remained in use after the grouping. The front of the card is simply a record of the work performed and the reference to 'As Booked' suggests it was used as a way of confirming if there had been any alterations to the booked work. The reverse side of the card concentrates upon shunting performed and which department requested the work to be undertaken, whilst at the bottom of the card there was space to record the names of the driver and fireman and hours worked, and to the right of the card there was space for recording what coal and oil was obtained while they were away from their home station.

1. The first example is dated 11/7/1929 and is for No. 183 Driver J. Cookson, who was stationed at Carlisle. He appears to have booked on at 3.0 p.m. and was engaged in stabling engines on the shed, giving the numbers of three Compounds, Nos. 1137, 1144, 1147, a Class 3F 0–6–0T No. 16368, a 4–4–0 No. 14462 and an 0–6–0 No. 17688. He booked off at 11.0 p.m. having completed an eight-hour day.

I have been been able to find pictures of several of the locomotives that are mentioned in these notes, beginning with those that were marshalled on shed during the unnamed driver's shift on 1st July 1929. Three Standard Compounds are recorded and I have included views of Nos. 1137 and 1144. The picture of No. 1137 illustrates what was probably a locomotive that had not been in service very long and may even have been ex-works; note the absence of a shedplate.

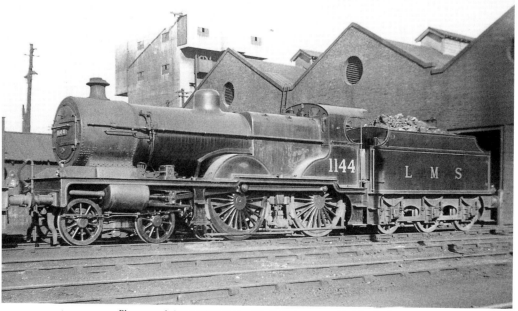

The other Compound is No. 1144 seen here when photographed at Kingmoor in May 1938.
COLLECTION R. J. ESSERY

Pictures of three other locomotives that were stabled by J. Cookson will be found on pages 48 & 49.

L. M. & S. R.

Date 11/7 192 9   Station **bc**   Engine No. _____   Turn No. _____

PARTICULARS OF SHUNTING PERFORMED.

(Shunting by Train Engines includes marshalling and disposing of train and attaching and detaching on Journey. The whole of the time from commencing shunting operations until engine is coupled to train ready to resume journey to be charged as shunting.) **If no shunting performed write " NONE."**
Drivers of Shunting Engines to state intervals for meals and locomotive duties.

Shunting at	TIME.				Department for	COAL & OIL.
	From	To	Hrs.	Mts.		If obtained at an outlying coalstage or wagon (away from a shed); or from another Company's depot state:
						Coal: (Cwts.) _____
						Oil: (pts.) _____
						Where obtained } _____

When Journal cannot be made out by Driver he must enter particulars as below:—

DRIVER.		FIREMAN.		Stationed at	Engine Hours.	Late Start with first trip. H. M.	Late arr. with last trip. H. M.	Time liberated from train	Time arr. on ashpit.
No.	Name.	No.	Name.						
188	Jns Cookson			bc					

Where relieved _____   Time _____ m.   Relief Driver stationed at _____

L. M. & S. R.

P. F. 1189. 2/25.

Date 11/7 192 9   Station **bc**   Turn No. _____

Particulars of deviations from Booked Working, and Additional Trips Worked.

If all trips as scheduled on Job Card were worked write " As Booked " and initial the Card.

Dep. Time.	From	To	Arrival time.	Route via.	Description of Train.	Loaded, Empty, L. E. or E. & V.
	Stabled engines					
	1147	1144	1137	17688		
	16368	14462				
				Booked on 3 Ro		
				op 116w		

The front and reverse sides of the Enginemen's Record Card as described on page 46.

The final locomotive was No. 17688, a Pickersgill 0—6—0, one of a class of forty-three that were built between 1918 and 1920. Classified as 3F by the LMS, twenty-nine were still in service at Nationalization.

A. G. ELLIS

The other locomotives were all ex-Caledonian and we begin with No. 16368, a McIntosh engine now classified as 3F by the LMS. The locomotive stock number was badly faded, but both the '3' and the '8' are visible.
A. G. ELLIS

The next locomotive to be mentioned is a Pickersgill 4—4—0 No. 14462, seen in this 1931 picture at Carlisle station. This class was built between 1916 and 1922 and all survived to become British Railways locomotives.
J. A. G. H. COLTAS

L. M. & S. R.

Date _4 July_ 192_9_ Engine No. _14615_ Station _Carlisle_ Turn No. _103_

PARTICULARS OF SHUNTING PERFORMED.

(Shunting by Train Engines includes marshalling and disposing of train and attaching and detaching on Journey. The whole of the time from commencing shunting operations until engine is coupled to train ready to resume Journey to be charged as shunting.) If no shunting performed write " NONE."
Drivers of Shunting Engines to state intervals for meals and locomotive duties.

| Shunting at | TIME. | | | | Department for |
	From	To	Hrs.	Mts.	
Mid	7-15a	7-50a		35	Goods

COAL & OIL.

If obtained at an outlying coalstage or wagon (away from a shed) ; or from another Company's depot state:

Coal: (Cwts.) ....

Oil: (pts.) ....

Where obtained } ....

When Journal cannot be made out by Driver he must enter particulars as below :—

| DRIVER. | | FIREMAN. | | Stationed at | Engine Hours. | Late Start with first trip. | | Late arr. with last trip. | | Time liberated from train | Time arr. on ashpit. |
No.	Name.	No.	Name.			H.	M.	H.	M.		
629	Haddow	311	S Wigham	Cle						7-50a	8-15a

Where relieved .... Time .... m. Relief Driver stationed at ....

L. M. & S. R.

P. F. 1188.
2/25.

Date _4 July_ 192_9_ Station _Carlisle_ Turn No. _103_

Particulars of deviations from Booked Working, and Additional Trips Worked.

If all trips as scheduled on Job Card were worked write "As Booked" and initial the Card.

Dep. Time.	From	To	Arrival time.	Route via.	Description of Train.	Loaded, Empty, L. E. or E. & V.
6-55a	Exchange	Mid	7-15a			41 etrs
7-50a	Mid	Shops	8-15a			L. E.
	Book on 11-50 pm		Book on 11-50 pm			
	off 8-30a		off 8-30a			

The front and reverse sides of the Enginemen's Record Card for Turn 103, as described opposite.

No 14615 was the locomotive working Turn 103 on 4th July and during the day was booked as spending 35 minutes shunting at 'Mid' for the Goods Dept. The locomotive was an ex-G&SWR Drummond design, one of six built during 1914-15 and later rated as Class 3P by the LMS. This picture was taken at Kingsmoor on 16th September 1929, shortly after Driver Haddow made the record of the work undertaken. The class was extinct by 1937.
J. I. RUTHERFORD

2. The second card is dated 4th July and covers Turn No. 103 with a 4–6–0 No. 14615 which went from Exchange Sidings departing at 6.55 a.m. with 41 empties and arriving at 'Mid' (presumably somewhere on the Midland Division) at 7.15 a.m. The next 35 minutes were spent shunting at 'Mid' for the Goods Department. The driver was No. 62 G. Haddow and his fireman was No. 311 S. Wigham. The return trip was light engine, departing at 7.50 a.m. to Shups, arriving at the ashpit at 8.15 a.m. The men had booked on at 11.50 p.m. and booked off at 8.30 a.m. This tends to suggest that each job was detailed on a separate card, rather than having a single written record for the entire shift.

3. The third card covers some relief work undertaken in Glasgow on 3rd July 1929. The enginemen were No. 85 Driver Hutcheson and No. 263 Fireman W. Pasker who relieved the men on an 0–6–0 No. 17570, which was working the 7.15 a.m. freight train from Carlisle. Relief took place at 4.40 p.m. at a junction in Glasgow (the name is not legible) and they worked the loaded freight train forward to Glasgow College, arriving at 4.45 p.m. Following arrival, the engine was uncoupled and at 4.55 p.m. they went light engine to St. Enoch locomotive shed, arriving at 5.5 p.m. Note the card shows 10 minutes booked to shunting time at College.

SALTMARKET JCT.

My initial comment was that the old Midland system, adopted by the LMS, to use a '.' for a.m. and a '/' for p.m., made a lot of sense. I assume the clerks who dealt with these records were used to the driver's writing and 'shorthand', but it is not easy to understand if you are not familiar with the area. My assumption is that they are Caledonian cards as used during the post-1923 period, but I await further comments from readers.

The 7.15 a.m. freight train from Carlisle was worked by a McIntosh 0–6–0 No. 175700, one of a class built between 1899 and 1909 by the Caledonian Railway. The class was longlived, all became British Railways stock, and the final withdrawal did not take place until 1963.
A. G. ELLIS

L. M. & S. R.

Date 3-7- 1929 Engine No. 17570   Station St Enoch   Turn No. 80

PARTICULARS OF SHUNTING PERFORMED.

(Shunting by Train Engines includes marshalling and disposing of train and attaching and detaching on Journey. The whole of the time from commencing shunting operations until engine is coupled to train ready to resume journey to be charged as shunting.) **If no shunting performed write "NONE."**
Drivers of Shunting Engines to state intervals for meals and locomotive duties.

COAL & OIL.

Shunting at	From	To	Hrs	Mts.	Department for
College				10	

If obtained at an outlying coalstage or wagon (away from a shed); or from another Company's depot state:

Coal: (Cwts.) ....

Oil: (pts.) ....

Where obtained }

When Journal cannot be made out by Driver he must enter particulars as below:—

DRIVER.		FIREMAN.		Stationed at	Engine Hours.	Late Start with first trip. H. M.	Late arr. with last trip. H. M.	Time liberated from train	Time arr. on ashpit.
No.	Name.	No.	Name.						
85	Hutchison	263	W. Parker					4 55	5 5

Where relieved .... Time .... m. Relief Driver stationed at ....

L. M. & S. R.

P. F. 1189. 2/25

Date 3-7- 1929 Station St Enoch   Turn No. 80   111

Particulars of deviations from Booked Working, and Additional Trips Worked.

If all trips as scheduled on Job Card were worked write "As Booked" and initial the Card.

Dep. Time.	From	To	Arrival time.	Route via.	Description of Train.	Loaded, Empty, L. E. or E. & V.
4 30	Saltmarket J 1	College	4 45		Freight	Loaded
4 5	College	St Enoch Loco	5 5			L. E.
	Relieved men of 7 15 ex Carlisle					

The front and reverse sides of the third Enginemen's Record Card as described on page 51. A picture of the locomotive working Turn 80 is opposite.

Between the wars, the railways were keen to capture the growing traffic in bulk milk carried in rail tankers, but churn traffic was still important. This Bedford flatbed was conveying a load of the later type of churns with parallel sides, in contrast to the older tapered type. In an age before farmers had lorries of their own, these arrangements were particularly important for the rapid collection of milk for conveyance to the railway. The location was possibly the Peak District.
COLLECTION NELSON TWELLS

ROAD CARTAGE on the Somerset & Dorset Line

by NEIL BURGESS

In previous articles[1] I have outlined how the LMS, in concert with the Southern Railway, attempted to modernise and improve the viability of the Somerset & Dorset Joint line, which the two companies had inherited from their Midland and London & South Western constituents respectively, and for which the LMS had assumed day-to-day responsibility from 1930. Those articles dealt principally with the operation of the rail services over the line; but from an early stage in their histories railway companies had provided a variety of road transport systems for the carriage of passengers and goods which were intended to feed into their railway operations. The development of independent road transport undertakings, mostly set up to compete directly with the railways, had increased considerably with the end of the Great War, not least because many men in the armed forces during that conflict had learned to drive and chose to invest their savings in the former military lorries sold off in considerable numbers after 1919. Like most hauliers, the railways had made extensive use of horse traction in the pre-war period, but pressure from competitors and the need to make use of the labour-saving and efficiency potential of internal combustion machines, not least in the face of the Great Depression after 1929, led to large-scale reorganisation of their road transport operations in the interwar years.

On 22nd June 1934, a report on road cartage in connection with the Somerset & Dorset line was presented to the Joint Officers' meeting. The report had been compiled by H. W. Faircloth and P. W. Jones for the LMS and A. E. Hammett and G. F. Lockhart for the Southern and is contained in the minutes of the Joint Officers' meeting in the National Archives at Kew.[2] This article sets out the contents of the report and seeks to understand the light they cast on the operation of the joint line during the 1930s.

Table 1: Summary of Road Vehicles operated from Joint Committee stations

Location	Provision of vehicles*	Provision of stabling	Traffic for 12-week period to 24/3/1934	Area covered [radius]	Notes
Blandford	1 2-ton motor 2 horses 2 horse vehicles	2 sets	1,394 tons	10 miles	replaced a 5-ton motor from June 1933 1 set of stables let out An extra horse vehicle provided after June 1933
Bridgwater	1 2-ton motor 1 horse 3 horse vehicles	1 set	1,070 tons	8 miles	1 horse trolley surplus to requirements
Evercreech New	Provided by cartage agent since 1909	none	not stated	not stated	agent [R. C. Green] a former signalman
Glastonbury	2 2-ton motors 1 4-ton motor 1 1-ton motor	used as a garage	1,884 tons	10 miles	replacement for 2-ton motor from 1933
Highbridge & Burnham	1 2-ton motor	occupied by shunting horses	373 tons	10 miles	no provision for handling container traffic
Radstock & Midsomer Norton	1 2-ton motor	let out	718 tons	5 miles	motor allocation augmented from Bristol as required
Shepton Mallett	1 2-ton motor 1 covered tilt	let out	407 tons	8 miles	surplus to requirements
Shillingstone	1 2-ton motor	none	507 tons	12 miles	motor assists at Sturminster Newton and Blandford as required
Stalbridge	Provided by cartage agent	none	not stated	not stated	
Sturminster Newton	1 2-ton motor	let out	612 tons	13 miles	assists with traffic at Stalbridge as required
Wells	1 2-ton motor	let out as a garage	704 tons	10 miles	
Wincanton	1 horse vehicle	2 stalls	329 tons	not stated	
West Pennard	1 2-ton motor	none	364 tons	not stated	vehicle introduced from 2nd January 1934; assists at Glastonbury, Bridgwater and Wells as required

*All motors were built by Karrier and fitted with pneumatic tyres apart from one 2-ton Karrier with solid tyres each at Glastonbury and West Pennard; and a 6-wheeled Morris at Glastonbury.

CARTAGE PROVISION ON THE JOINT LINE PRIOR TO THE REPORT

The report contains two appendices, 'A' and 'B', from which it is possible to extract details of the road cartage situation prevailing immediately prior to the compilation of the report. According to Appendix A, the provision of vehicles at the various stations was as shown in *Table 1*.

Table 1 illustrates the preponderance of motor vehicles in use by the Joint Committee, reflecting their greater usefulness in rural areas compared to horses. That a number of railway stables had been let out, some for other uses entirely, indicates that the Joint Committee could see no general change in this overall trend; however, there is an interesting note in Appendix A which indicates that the railway operators were not thinking of disposing of stabling altogether:

'In regard to the 8-stall stable [at Shepton Mallett], co-incident with our visit a Mr Swain of Woodlands Farm, Shepton Mallett, was making enquiry as to whether the stables and land adjacent thereto would be suitable for use as a piggery. Mr Swain inspected the buildings and stated he would consider the matter further after consulting the Local Sanitary Officer when he will communicate with the Stationmaster. We think there is a possible tenant in Mr Swain and the Estate Agent has been placed in possession of the facts'.[3]

Even so, the days of horse cartage in such rural areas was not over, as illustrated by a discussion in the main body of the report:

'It is considered there is a possibility of developing additional business at Wincanton by the introduction of a mechanical unit in place of the horse unit, in order that service may be offered over a much wider radius, and we recommend that this be authorised.
'At Sturminster Newton only one motor vehicle is employed to cover local deliveries, radial distances up to 13 miles, also assisting as required at Stalbridge and Henstridge stations. The important village of Marnhull is only served occasionally and we are of the opinion that additional traffics would be secured if a daily delivery was arranged.
'In order that an experiment may be made in this direction we recommend that a single horse unit be provided for local cartage work, thus releasing the motor for country deliveries and to assist at other neighbouring stations as required.'[4]

OPERATIONAL COSTS AND REVENUES

The report as a whole is generally couched in positive terms about the Joint Committee's cartage operations. The opening paragraph of the main text says:

'The weight carted during the period examined shews an increase of 21.8% over the previous year, and the average cost per ton 3s 2.95d compared with 3s 6.68d, a decrease of 3.73d. In regard to this we particularly desire to commend the Station Masters at Blandford, Shillingstone and Sturminster Newton, whom, we are satisfied, are largely responsible for the improvement in traffic at these stations.[5]

Appendix B provides a detailed analysis of operational costs at the Joint Committee stations from which cartage was conducted and this is set out in *Table 2*.
Overall, the figures in *Table 2* point to a 21.8% increase in tonnage dealt with for an

Table 2: Summary of Cartage costs at Joint Committee stations[6]

Station	Cost of operating ★	Mileage ★	Tonnage ★	Cost per ton ★
Blandford	£153. 4. 3	1,328	768	3s. 11.88d
	£175. 1.11	2,918	1,394	2s. 6.15d
Bridgwater	£135.19. 1	1,732	1,002	2s. 8.56d
	£139.11. 7	1,751	1,070	2s. 7.31d
Glastonbury	£340.17.11	8,216	1,785	3s. 9.83d
	£352.15. 1	7,979	1,884	3s. 8.94d
Highbridge	£100. 0. 8	2,649	588	3s. 4.83d
	£94. 5. 2	2,616	575	3s. 3.34d
Radstock	£117. 2. 6	2,534	732	3s. 2.40d
	£118.19.10	2,164	718	3s. 3.77d
Shepton Mallett	£87. 3. 4	1,828	381	4s. 6.91d
	£83. 4. 6	1,693	407	4s. 1.08d
Shillingstone	£90. 0. 9	2,823	458	3s. 11.18d
	£84. 7. 2	2,833	507	3s. 3.93d
Sturminster Newton	£86. 5. 0	2,272	505	3s. 4.99d
	£92. 8. 9	3,011	612	3s. 0.25d
Wells	£96.18. 3	2,743	610	3s. 2.13d
	£90. 6. 0	2,476	704	2s. 6.78d
West Pennard	n/s	n/s	n/s	n/s
	£97. 8. 7	2,250	364	5s. 4.24d
Wincanton	£42.15. 4	n/s	202	4s. 2.81d
	£61.11.10	n/s	329	3s. 8.93d
totals	£1,250	–	7,031	3s. 6.68d
	£1,390	–	8,564	3s. 2.95d

★ In each case the first figure is the cost of operating in 1933 adjusted in real terms at 1934 rates along with mileages run and tonnage conveyed in 1933: the second figure is the actual operational costs, plus mileage and tonnage, for the twelve-week survey period to 24th March 1934.

11.2% increase in real operating costs; and a net reduction of 8.74% in operating costs per ton carried. One of the reasons for this is that, in the years following the Depression of 1929–31, most western economies suffered from deflation; in other words, a progressive increase in the real value of money. Thus, despite the difficulties of maintaining a business in the face of falling demand and financial stringency, those which could keep going actually benefited from the effects of deflation. 1934 was a point in the world economy when these benefits were still being felt; with the later 1930s as economies picked up and deflation turned towards inflation, not least in reaction to the need for re-armament, they disappeared.

LOCAL REALITIES

As *Table 1* indicates, not all the cartage from Joint Line stations was in the hands of the railway. Appendix A to the report outlined the situation at Evercreech New and indicates that arrangements were not always in the Joint Committee's favour:

'The cartage service at this station has been performed by a cartage Agent, Mr R. C. Green, since 1909 who, prior to taking over this work, was a signalman employed by the Joint Committee.
'It was suggested in the report dated 28th March 1934, called for by the Southern and LM&S Conference [min. 426 19th January 1934] that the Cartage Agent should be displaced and the work taken over by a "mechanical horse" and trailer and to also take over the necessary cartage requirements at Evercreech Junction and Pylle.
'On investigation we find that Mr Green, who is said to be about 70 years of age, has created during the time of his agency a very close relationship with the local traders and general public and there is little doubt that, in the event of this proposal being carried out, he is in a position to secure standing orders for the cartage of the principal traffics, also to alienate the relations of the traders with the Railway Companies.
'In addition to the single horse unit employed by the Agent, it is frequently necessary for him to call upon his two sons, who are in the road haulage business, to render assistance in carting traffic to and from the station.
'There would appear to be very little opportunity of the development of business in this district from the fact that the principal traffics passing by throughout road transport consist of grain and other feeding stuffs from Bristol and Avonmouth which are conveyed at rates of 5s 10d and 6s 0d per ton respectively compared to our very low delivered

rate of 7s 6d per ton within a radius of 3 miles of destination station. Having regard to all the circumstances we are of the opinion that during the lifetime of the Agent it would not be politic with the Committee to interfere with the present arrangements.'[7]

FUTURE PLANS
Seven proposals were set out in the main body of the report:

Mechanical Horse Tractors
We have considered the proposal of the District Goods and Passenger Manager as set out on page 12 of the LM&S Company's Chief Officers' report dated 28th March 1934, for 3-ton Scammell Cob Tractors to be placed at various stations on the Joint Line, and in regard thereto we have incorporated our recommendations in Appendix 'A' which are summarised thus:

Evercreech New	Displacing Cartage Agent at Evercreech New, and also to cover country lorry deliveries from Evercreech Junction and Pylle.	No alteration at present
Wincanton	For extended deliveries, one horse team and hired cartage to be displaced.	Recommended
Bridgwater	-do-	No alteration at present
Glastonbury	Displacing 2 ton motor	Recommended in place of 4-ton motor
Highbridge	Displacing 2-ton motor	No alteration at present
Blandford	Displacing two single horse drays	Recommended in place of 2-ton motor

Closer Working with the Great Western Railway
In regard to the proposal for closer working with the Great Western Railway at Bridgwater, Highbridge, Burnham and Wells, which matter is being considered by another Committee, we recommend that no alteration be made in the present cartage plant pending a definite decision on this subject, other than to meet traffic requirements as they arise, eg. the provision of a horse lurry for container traffic at Highbridge.[8]

MISCELLANEOUS MATTERS
There were a number of miscellaneous matters in the report. One concerned the completion of worknotes, probably a term for daily worksheets, which, the report noted, were not receiving proper attention and were not being completed on the day the work was done: 'The position in this respect at Bridgwater is particularly unsatisfactory'.

The Southern Railway had installed two petrol 'storage bins' – presumably tanks – at Sturminster Newton and another at Shillingstone, which were to be charged to the Joint committee; further bins were to be provided by the LMS. However, the processes for issuing petrol were described as 'not in all cases

satisfactory' as drivers had access to supplies and station masters were to be reminded that they needed to authorise supplies in future.

The LMS had also supplied a number of vehicles for use on the Joint line and these bore the company's livery and lettering; it was felt desirable that the Joint Committee's name should appear on all vehicles in use at its stations.

THE CONSTANT SEARCH FOR OPERATIONAL ECONOMIES
In the previous articles alluded to, I suggested that the LMS had, on effectively assuming day-to-day control of the Somerset & Dorset line in 1930, undertaken a persistent search for more economic methods of operation. This discussion indicates that the search included rail-related road haulage undertaken by the Joint Committee and that here there were various opportunities not only for more economical operation, but also expansion of the business by the employment of internal combustion engine-powered vehicles which possessed not only greater range but also versatility which horse-drawn vehicles lacked. Even redundant stabling, originally provided for cartage horses, might be turned to profit, though quite what effect on the station at Shepton Mallett a piggery might have is a fine question.

Even so, the question of how best to deal with Mr Green, the former signalman turned carrier at Evercreech New, illustrates the ways in which the Joint Committee – and no doubt railway operators of road transport elsewhere – might be made hostages to fortune as a result of long-standing arrangements. No doubt the Joint Committee might have thought in 1909 that giving business to a former

employee was both an economical arrangement and also, given his presumed loyalty to his old employers, a beneficial one. But the passage of time and the growth of other local loyalties had shifted the balance in favour of Mr Green, who, with his sons, was in a position that the Joint Committee thought it imprudent to challenge.

By 1934 the worst of the Great Depression was over in much of the country, though the old industrial areas of the midlands and the north were still badly affected. Having weathered the economic blizzard of 1929–31, the railways, though by no means out of difficulties, were able to have modest confidence that receipts were on the increase, that new technology might come to their assistance as well as help their rivals and that the effects of deflation in monetary values might give them a helping hand as well.

Footnotes
[1] 'Making Economies on the Somerset & Dorset, 1929–31': in *LMS Journal* No. 6 and 'Pursuing Further Economies on the Somerset & Dorset 1931–4?': in *LMS Journal* No. 29
[2] RAIL 626/29
[3] Appendix A, p.3
[4] Main report, p.1
[5] Main report, p.1
[6] All figures from Appendix B, p.2
[7] Appendix A, p.1
[8] Main report, p.2

A further picture of a lorry used by the LMS will be found on page 58 and I am obliged to Nelson Twells for supplying them.　　Editor

Although neither of these photographs show vehicles used for cartage in connection with the Somerset & Dorset line, they do illustrate types of vehicle commonly used on the LMS system, though some years later than those mentioned in the article. This is a two-ton Dennis flatbed lorry, sometimes referred to as a 'flying pig', possibly because the bonnet suggests a snout. The bodywork for these vehicles was built by the manufacturer, rather than the railway company, as had been the case with earlier lorries. This view was taken during wartime judging by the hooded headlamps and white-lined mudguards, and it seems to have been converted to run on gas, the apparatus for which was mounted behind the cab. However, the photograph is useful in showing the varied loads carried by these light delivery vehicles, which here included two trunks, wicker baskets, packing cases and a couple of metal drums. The tarpaulin for covering the load had been folded and stowed on top of the large basket marked '32'. It is believed that in later years the Somerset & Dorset Joint Committee operated lorries of this type, possibly replacements for the 2-ton Karrier types referred to in the article.

COLLECTION NELSON TWELLS

Handling the Passenger

In today's world, people who travel by train and were known as passengers are called 'customers'; they travel to and from 'train stations', the old name 'railway station' is no longer used. Station Managers, not Station Masters, are in charge and so on. Do we have a better railway system? That is for readers to decide, but I felt an insight into how the LMS taught their staff to handle the passenger would be of interest. This article is based upon a section of Passenger Station Working, *one of the handbooks used by the LMS at their School of Transport where the company's staff was taught what today we would call 'best practice.' The book was published in August 1938.*

Bob Essery.

RECEPTION

The reception of passenger traffic may be defined as the passage of the traveller from the highway to the railway carriage. In Great Britain it is the practice for this to take place at a station or halt. Reception of special kinds is met from time to time, as in the case of stations serving docks or airports, but most passengers reach the station on foot or by road vehicle.

Stations are provided with access for road vehicles. At stations in large towns this feature may assume great importance, and the accommodation for unloading taxis and motor cars should be adequate to cope with the heaviest arrival flows without delay. In such a case it is probable that the entrance and exit will be so arranged that a vehicle, after unloading, will proceed back to the highway without fouling the route of arriving loaded vehicles, thus maintaining a continuous and unidirectional flow of vehicles. Similarly the entrances for pedestrians should be wide enough to accommodate the traffic at peak periods without congestion.

In consequence of the modern reluctance of people to walk, many reach a station by omnibus and in order to reduce the distance they may have to walk from the 'bus to the station, arrangements have been made in certain instances for the vehicles working the services to utilise the station forecourt either as a stopping place or as a terminus. In other instances we have been successful in inducing passenger road transport undertakings to arrange their services so as to stop opposite the stations or in close proximity thereto.

Porters take charge of passengers' luggage on arrival at the station. At large stations it is usual for porters to be constantly in attendance at the entrance, especially before the departure of the principal trains. What the porters do with the passengers' luggage is described in Chapter II, but they attend personally to the passengers until they are seated in the train. Passengers arriving on foot have usually little or no luggage, and make their own way to the train.

To receive passengers at some large stations commissionaires have been appointed. At holiday times, at certain stations, 'passengers' friends' are appointed, capable members of the station staff, whose title is descriptive of their duties.

Before leaving the station entrance it may be noted that, wherever possible, the Railway Company provides a space where passengers and others may park their cars. Accommodation for cycles is available in the left luggage offices, and regular passengers can obtain season tickets covering deposit of their cycles or cars at any time while the station is open.

After arrival at the station, the passengers' first action is usually to buy their tickets, if they have not booked in advance. The Booking Office is placed in a position convenient in relation to the entrance. At large stations having more than one entrance, there are often one or more additional booking offices.

Time bills and special notices about trains should be displayed in the vicinity of the station entrance and booking office so that passengers may be confronted with essential and useful information. To facilitate reference a red line should be drawn under the name of the station at which sheet timetables are exhibited and the times shown opposite it, wherever the station's name occurs in the time sheets; the red line should extend right across the table.

Obstacles to the free flow of passengers from the highway to the trains should be avoided. The shorter the distance and the fewer the obstructions, the quicker will the passengers be passed through the approaches to the platforms. Only in this way is it possible to clear the passengers at peak-periods with a minimum of accommodation. This may seem unconnected with the conditions at country stations, but even the country station may find its facilities taxed on the occasion of a local carnival, fête, or flower show.

Many passengers reach stations before their trains arrive or are set at the platform. For these it is necessary to provide waiting rooms, seats in suitable places, and lavatories. At the chief termini, dealing with trains whose journeys last the greater part of a day or night, there may also be bathrooms and hairdressing saloons. Passengers may wish to leave their baggage in safe custody; for this there is a left luggage office or cloak room. Passengers may also have business at the station master's office; if they are making several consecutive journeys, it may be a convenience to have telegrams and correspondence addressed 'c/o. Station Master'.

In addition to the necessary facilities associated with the reception of passengers, the following are often provided for travellers' convenience:

Pillar boxes,
Telephone call-boxes,
Telegraph facilities,
Bookstalls, Stalls for tobacco, fruit and sweets,
Automatic machines for cigarettes, chocolates, &c.

At the largest stations, some postal facilities may be provided, and a chemist's shop. The siting of these shops, stalls, and kiosks must be conveniently near the principal routes of access to the station, without being so placed that their patrons will cause congestion of circulating areas, or impede the free flow of passengers.

It is not generally necessary to provide spare space at the point where road vehicles unload or in the booking hall, because each passenger alights, passes on to buy his ticket, and passes on again as quickly as possible.

At large termini it is usual to provide a concourse, an open space of considerable area, from which departure platforms are separated by ticket barriers. Many of the facilities mentioned, waiting rooms, refreshment rooms, shops, stalls and kiosks, may have access from the concourse with advantage to the passenger and the revenue earning facilities concerned, but the primary object of the concourse is to be a means whereby all the passengers may pass quickly from any entrance to any platform, without confusion and congestion. Therefore, the multiplication of non-railway facilities on the concourse requires careful control.

The desirability of free movement applies at the ticket barriers as elsewhere. It is necessary that a check be imposed on people obtaining access to the platforms, and a ticket barrier is provided for this purpose at most stations of any size, but it is desirable to provide sufficient gates and staff to prevent passengers being blocked back into the concourse or booking hall.

Having passed the ticket barrier, the reception of the passenger is almost at an end. Little more can be done for him, when seated in the train, than that the boy selling magazines and papers, and the girl with sweets and fruit, should offer him a final chance of providing himself with some occupation for the journey.

DIRECTION BOARDS

To assist the free flow of passengers it is necessary to provide direction boards, showing clearly the way to the accommodation required by passengers, i.e. the Booking Office, Left Luggage Office, Waiting Rooms, Enquiry Offices, Refreshment Rooms, Platforms, &c. These should be fixed at such heights on the line of flow of passengers that they can be clearly visible, both by day and night, when crowds are passing through the station. The information given on the direction boards should be as brief as possible but should be such that passengers are left in no doubt as to the direction they are to take; for instance, boards showing 'To the up trains' or 'To the down trains' are not satisfactory unless they have added some of the destinations to be reached by the respective up and down trains. It is obvious that passengers requiring direction are those who either have not used the station before or else use it very infrequently and it must not be assumed that they have any knowledge of the line and the local circumstances.

The various offices and accommodation used by the public should have suitable indicator boards fixed outside, if possible at right angles to the normal flow of passengers, and the platforms should be clearly numbered.

TRAIN DEPARTURE INDICATORS

Many passengers, when they arrive at the station from which they are commencing their train journey, are already aware of the actual or the approximate time of the departure of the train by which they wish to travel, and in order that they may readily confirm this and ascertain the number of the platform from which the train will depart, it is the practice to provide, at the busier stations, train departure indicators. It is desirable that such an indicator should be the first thing to strike the eye of the passenger on his arrival inside the station so that enquiries of the staff may be reduced to a minimum and that the passage of the passenger to the departure platform may be assisted and delay with consequent congestion avoided. At large stations where there are more than one entrance, it is necessary to provide indicators at points where they can be seen by the passengers before they pass to the booking offices or the platforms.

The indicator must show the departure time of the train, the number of the platform from which it will depart and some information regarding the towns served by it in order that it may be identified by the passengers. In some cases it may be possible to show all the stations served by the train and its connections; in others, particularly in the case of long distance trains, it is only possible to show the principal towns and connections. As it is essential that the indicator may be easily seen and understood by the average passenger, the information it gives must be in large clear type and this requirement limits to some extent the amount of information which can be included.

The type of train indicator depends on the number of trains from the station, the number of different destinations to which they run and the number of people using the station. At small stations where trains run to a number of different destinations, the indicator may consist of a frame into which can be placed by the station staff painted boards showing the destination station of the train or the principal stations served by it, with slots into which the plat-

form number can be inserted, and a piece of slate on which the time of the next train can be chalked. Where there are fewer destinations to be shown, they may be painted upon the indicator itself and have fixed alongside a piece of slate on which can be chalked the platform numbers and the departure times. At more important stations, the roller type of indicator is used. This consists of a cabinet in which, affixed to two rollers, is a linen blind. On the blind are mounted printed sheets giving particulars, in the order of departure, of the departure time, principal stations served and the platform number for each train. The cabinet has a glass front through which a section of the blind is visible to the public. On the departure of each train, the information regarding the train is wound out of sight and towards the top roller and at the end of the day the blind is rewound on to the bottom roller. When, on special occasions, alterations are made in the time of departure, the towns served by, or the platform number for a particular train, it is necessary to affix to this type of indicator a small board giving either particulars of the alterations or bearing the words 'See special notices'. Hooks are provided on the front of these indicators for such boards so that they may be hung over any announcement shown on the blind. Notice boards showing the information in respect of the altered trains or of additional trains not included on the indicator have to be placed adjacent to the train departure indicators whenever they may be required. Train indicators are manipulated by the ticket collectors except at the large stations where a foreman or other member of the wages staff may be deputed to do this.

At large stations the train departure indicators are supplemented by train departure sheets, posted at points where the main indicators are not visible but where the public are likely to require information regarding train departure times and platform numbers. These train departure sheets are usually printed in poster form and show, in chronological order, particulars of the whole of the train departures from the station concerned on weekdays and Sundays. At stations with a number of departure platforms each with a separate entrance from the public concourse, it is advantageous to affix at the entrance, as soon as the platform is opened to passengers, a board showing the destination of the train.

At stations where there is a frequent service of trains to various destinations operating from one platform it is desirable to have on the platform some indication of the destination of the next train. These indicators may give, on a painted board or metal plate, simply the destination of the next train or they may be more elaborate, incorporating a clock face indicating the time of the train. In other cases the indicators may be electric and indicate by means of lights the time and/or destination of the next train. This latter type may be controlled from the station signal box whilst the manually operated signs are operated by the platform staff or, when placed at the entrance to the platform, by the ticket collectors stationed there. When the signs are operated by the station staff, the destinations are denoted in accordance with the timings and order of trains shown in the working time book. On occasions when it becomes necessary to depart from the working laid down, information regarding the running has to be obtained from the station signal box.

The object of these platform indicators is to reduce the number of enquiries of the platform staff enabling them to devote their time to their work with less interruption than would otherwise be possible, to speed up the loading of the trains by avoiding the necessity of the passengers having to ascertain after a train has entered the platform whether that particular train is the one by which they require to travel, and to reduce the risk of a passenger joining the wrong train. The particular type of platform indicator in use at a station is dependent on the number of people using the platforms and the frequency of the train service.

TRAIN ARRIVAL INDICATORS

At large terminal stations, where considerable numbers of people regularly await the arrival of friends on incoming trains, train arrival indicators are provided. It is necessary to show on these indicators the due arrival time, the station at which the train commenced its journey, and in the case of long distance trains, the principal stations served, together with an indication as to the running of the trains, i.e. whether 'on time' or, if not, the number of minutes late, and the number of the platform at which it will arrive. The indicator usually consists of removable boards to indicate the due arrival time and the description of the train with a slate on which can be chalked

'on time' or the number of minutes late and the platform number. In some cases small boards are inserted into slots, level with the train description, indicating the running of the train and the platform number.

Train arrival indicators are provided in order that persons meeting trains can ascertain the expected arrival time and the platform number without enquiring of the station staff and therefore, such indicators are fixed at points adjacent to the arrival platform in such positions that they can be easily seen by the public awaiting incoming trains. It is generally desirable that some indication of the running of a train should be given at least 30 minutes before the train is due and the indication has to be shown until the train actually arrives. This means that when a train is running very late it is necessary to show on the indicator the number of minutes late it is on leaving or passing some well known point on the line: for example, at Euston trains, may be shown on the indicator as x minutes late at Rugby. There must be easy communication between the staff responsible for working the indicator and the station signal box.

In the case of some large stations, where the cost of providing and working such an indicator as that mentioned above would not be justified, train arrival sheets are provided. These are printed in poster form and show for every train, in chronological order of arrival, the due arrival time, the station from which the train commenced its journey, or the principal stations served, and the number of the platform at which the train normally arrives. These posters, which are sometimes combined with the train departure sheets, mentioned previously, are exhibited at points where the public meeting trains are likely to congregate. These train departure sheets are supplemented in some cases by a notice affixed to a board outside the stationmaster's office, or the telegraph office, or in some prominent position near the arrival platforms. On this notice are written particulars of the principal trains and of their running, i.e. whether right time, or if not, the number of minutes late at the last convenient stop, or in the case of long distance non-stop trains, at the time of passing a convenient point. This information is wired from the point concerned.

The method adopted for giving particulars of train arrivals to the public at the various stations depends upon the demand for such information. Any of the afore-

mentioned methods may be adopted at one station whilst at another the demand may be so little that no special indication is necessary,

RESERVED SEATS, COMPARTMENTS AND SLEEPING BERTHS

The advance reservation of accommodation on trains is a facility given to the public primarily for commercial reasons and a full description of the method by which reservation is effected and the full means by which the reserved accommodation is indicated is given in the commercial manual. It may be mentioned here, however, that the reservation system does assist the Railway Company to provide sufficient and suitable accommodation on the trains concerned and is particularly useful in connection with the working from Euston and St. Pancras. The reservation clerks at these stations are in close touch with the Operating Department and when reservations in a particular train reach a high number, the Operating Department are advised and are able to take steps to increase the accommodations on all the trains,

As will be seen from the commercial manual 'seat attendants' are provided at stations where large numbers of seats are reserved and passengers requiring finding reserved seats are directed to the seat attendant. At stations where special seat attendants are not provided, the porters on the platform assist passengers to find their reserved seats.

LOUD SPEAKERS

The adaption of the loud speaker to railway working is comparatively modern. An installation enables crowds of passengers to be directed and controlled much more effectively than can be done by any other means. Loud speakers are most useful when, at busy times, alterations in the timetable and the usual train platform arrangements become necessary. For instance, when trains are divided passengers can, if frequent suitable announcements are made, be directed to the correct portion of the train for their particular destination: if it becomes necessary to change the platform from which a train will leave after the passengers have already been admitted to the incorrect platform the transfer can be easily effected: passengers waiting on platforms for trains conveying a number of through vehicles to different destinations can be informed on what part of the platform they should wait: when breakdowns or severe delays occur, the public can be kept aware of the position.

Before a notice or series of notices is read, there should be some introductory statement such as 'This is Euston station' in order that the public may be quite sure the notice which they are about to hear is an authoritative one and also that they may be ready to listen to it. If the announcer suddenly commences with a public notice, it is probable that many people will not realise a statement which concerns them is being made until they have lost some vital part of the announcement. Loud speakers should not be used for unimportant notices which can satisfactorily be given by other means as a really important announcement would lose its appeal if sandwiched between comparatively trivial matters. For this reason it is necessary, at any rate at large stations, for the installation to be so arranged that groups of loud speakers may be cut out and not used for announcements which are unlikely to be of interest to the people congregated within their effective range. It must also be borne in mind in this connection that the view is often expressed that railway stations are already too noisy and it is undesirable to add needlessly to the noise, which, in addition to being distracting to the passengers, might, by reason of the position of the loud speakers, interfere with clerical work of the Company's staff.

It is necessary that care should be taken in choosing a man to act as announcer. He should be well spoken, with no marked peculiarity dialect and be able to read the statement he is required to make clearly and without hesitation. It must be borne in mind that the voice is amplified many times and therefore it is important to have an announcer with a voice suited to the microphone so that when it has been amplified, and possibly distorted somewhat in the process, is pleasant and easy to follow.

It may be that men with these qualifications are not available as announcers and in such cases it is necessary to choose first of all the man whose voice amplifies well and who in addition possesses some of the requirements, and then to endeavour to overcome by explanation and practice, the defects.

The station master or some responsible member of the staff delegated by him must decide what statements are to be made by means of the loud speakers, the time for the first and last readings and the frequency with which they are to be given. Formulae for all the various types of notices likely to be required should be carefully drafted and the staff concerned trained to read them distinctly and in a suitable manner. If this is done, there will be no difficulty, when it is considered necessary at short notice to make announcements by means of the loud speaker equipment, in having an appropriate statement written out and announced in a proper manner.

In the train departure announcements, the various stations served by the train should be given in the same way as shown on the departure indicators. When train arrivals are being announced, and trains are running late, no reference should be made to the late running; the statement should merely give particulars of the train, the expected arrival time and the platform number. All announcements must be as brief as possible and care must be taken to avoid ambiguity.

Standing instructions, setting out the important train departures which are to be announced daily, together with information regarding the time at which announcements should be made, can be given to the announcers. At busy periods, however, and when special trains are running, additional announcements become necessary. Many required at these periods can be prepared sometime in advance of the time for announcement but when large numbers of people are using the station it may be necessary to make announcements at short notice. In order that this may be done, there is at the large stations, telephonic communication from strategic points on the station to the announcer so that those responsible for the working may be able to inform him whenever special information should be broadcast. The announcer should keep a record of all such telephonic instructions. In those cases where it is not practicable to provide this telephonic communication, special arrangements will have to be made at the holiday peak periods for the conveyance of messages to the announcer.

CROWD PSYCHOLOGY– NEGATIVE INFORMATION

It often happens that at times when the service is disorganised, it may be owing to weather conditions, mishap, or heavy holiday traffic, large crowds are congregated at a busy station. Some people may be waiting to commence their journey whilst others have friends arriving by trains which are very late. Even after the due departure or arrival times of the various trains have passed it may be impossible to give definite positive information on their working. In such cases any information at all, for example, that a particular train will not arrive or depart before a certain time, is valuable and should be passed on to those waiting. The complete absence of news often results in people becoming difficult to handle with the possibility of crowds getting out of control, but if some information, which may be entirely negative, is passed to them they will appreciate that the authorities are endeavouring to help and are not keeping them 'in the dark'. Announcements of regret for delays in these exceptional circumstances and some suitable explanation of the reason or cause with, if appropriate, suggestions of alternative means of travel, can also do much to lessen public annoyance and assist in keeping crowds in order and good temper.

FORMATION OF QUEUES

When crowds are congregating in the booking hall or concourse for special excursion trains or travel in connection with special events, it is necessary for these intending passengers to be marshalled into queues, those holding tickets direct to the platform entrances and those requiring tickets to the booking office windows. When more than one booking office window is in use queues for each window should be formed and staff should be set apart to direct the people going into the station to the correct queue. The station master must depute a senior member of the staff to see that the best is done in this way to avoid congestion in the booking hall and concourse. The possibility of large crowds using the station can often be foreseen and special arrangements made in advance to deal with the traffic by having more booking clerks on duty, so that additional booking windows may be opened, more ticket collectors to man the entrances to the platforms, and more staff to control and regulate the queues which may form.

At these times of exceptional pressure of traffic it is necessary, at stations where trains convey a number of through vehicles to different destinations, to marshal the crowds on the platforms in suitable order so that loading into the train may be quickly accomplished and the conflicting movements of passengers on the platforms, when the train runs in, avoided, or at any rate reduced. It is sometimes possible in a similar way to marshal separately the first and third-class passengers. In cases where trains for different destinations are departing from the same platform within short intervals, it is desirable, if possible, to hold back from the platform the passengers for the second train until the first has departed. If this cannot be done, either because of pressure on accommodation off the platform, or because of the short interval between the trains, efforts must be made to marshal those passengers for the next train at the front of the platform and those for subsequent trains behind. In any case if it is seen that a platform is likely to become dangerously overcrowded, it is absolutely essential that further people be prevented from gaining access to it.

HANDLING DIFFERENT TYPES OF PASSENGERS

It will have been seen from the foregoing that it is necessary in handling the public to regard every passenger or prospective passenger as having no knowledge whatever of the layout of the particular station, the trains, or the usual methods of railway working. Such arrangements must be made that the answer to every question which is likely to be raised can be satisfactorily ascertained by the passenger with little trouble either to himself or to the Company's staff. Everything possible must be done to render the passage from the station entrance to the train, with the various intermediate formalities, easy and expeditious.

In making the various arrangements in this connection, it must be borne in mind that the regular daily passengers (residential traffic) require less attention and direction than do all other types of travellers. They proceed to and from the trains quickly and provided there is no interruption in the usual arrangements no very great difficulty, except what may be due to the actual numbers travelling in relation to the capacity of the station, is experienced.

Business travellers are accustomed to travel by trains but may not use a particular station regularly and therefore require more assistance at the station. They make greater use of the various facilities provided and consequently their passage to and from the trains takes longer. The position is much different with non-business travellers who are often unused to rail travel and require direction and advice constantly from the time they enter the station premises at the commencement of their journey until they leave at the completion.

Excursion passengers travelling at very low fares do not require quite the same attention as some of the other types of passengers. They will all be travelling by one train or a group of special trains and can therefore be easily directed. As a rule they do not make extensive use of the various facilities provided at the station and they can usually be segregated quite easily from the other types of passengers. The handling of excursion passengers travelling in large parties is facilitated as instructions regarding travel can be given to them by the promoter or organiser before the journey. In cases where more than one train is required for such parties, distinctive coloured sets of tickets are used for each train and issued in bulk to the promoters for distribution. The trains are arranged to leave at varying times and the seating accommodation of each train coincides with the actual number of tickets issued for the particular train. In this way overcrowding of both the station and the train can be avoided.

The requirements of the transfer passengers must not be overlooked at junction and exchange stations and suitable direction boards and other facilities must be provided and arrangements made for their easy passage from train to train.

ENQUIRY OFFICES

At large stations, the public demand for information on train services and other travel matters may be so extensive that it cannot be dealt with satisfactorily by the booking clerks, ticket collectors and porters in addition to their normal work. In such cases enquiry offices are provided, staffed by clerks who are (or become) experienced in dealing with this particular business. Enquiry offices assist in the efficient handling of passengers at the large stations in the following ways:–

(a) Persons making enquiries are concentrated in an office away from the flow of traffic.

(b) Passengers can be directed to the trains or other offices required, thus making more rapid their passage through the station.

(c) The operating staff are relieved to a considerable extent from the necessity of interrupting their work to answer questions and obtain information for the passengers.

GENERAL

In these days of keen competition it is absolutely essential that everything be done for all types of passengers to ensure that all may have journeys free from worry and trouble so that they may look upon railway travel as something pleasant and worth while. In this connection it must not be overlooked that in addition to the competition with other forms of transport, there is competition for the spare cash of the public between railway transport and cinemas, theatres, radio, and other forms of entertainment and amusement.

For this reason 'Handling the passenger' becomes a matter of at least as great importance from the commercial as from the operating point of view.

Fig. 1 Part of the Railway Clearing House Junction Diagram for Liverpool.

LMS SIGNALS No. 28
Liverpool Exchange
Colour Light Re-signalling

by MICHAEL ADDISON, NOEL COATES, TONY GRAHAM, REG INSTONE & L. G. WARBURTON

In May 1946 the LMS commissioned an extensive installation of colour light signalling at Liverpool Exchange. This was the culmination of a number of proposals to renew and modernise the signalling there that was by then fifty years old and worn out.

The East Lancashire Railway reached a temporary station at Great Howard Street, Liverpool, via Bolton and Wigan on 20th November 1848. The way south was blocked by an arm of the Leeds and Liverpool Canal that required a 1:70 climb

over four iron spans leading to Tithebarn Street station that was some 25ft above the streets that ran beneath it, thus preventing further expansion.

The new station was opened by the Lancashire and Yorkshire Railway and the East Lancashire Railway on 15th May 1850, when it had five platform faces, one being for arrivals and two each for L&Y and ELR departures. In 1862 there were thirty-nine trains in and out of the station every twenty-four hours. In 1867 the Liverpool Corporation made suggestions with regard

to the redeveloping of streets around the station that led to the LYR applying for development to the east of the station and so, in 1876, plans were submitted to double the size of the station, but they were not proceeded with. In 1881 plans for the new station were invited, considered, and deemed unsatisfactory. This led to a second competition in 1882 from which a winning design was selected and approved. The main feature was the provision of a new canal basin east of the station, allowing the old arm to be removed and permitting a much

Plate 1. *Liverpool Exchange Station on 28th August 1921, showing roads 6 to 11 and the 'A' Box on the left that was numbered 424 in the L&YR list and of Railway Signal Company design with a brick base, built in 1886, containing 168 levers. Exchange 'A' box was renamed No. 2 box on the resignalling. The electrified lines on the right are those to Southport.*
L & Y SOCIETY

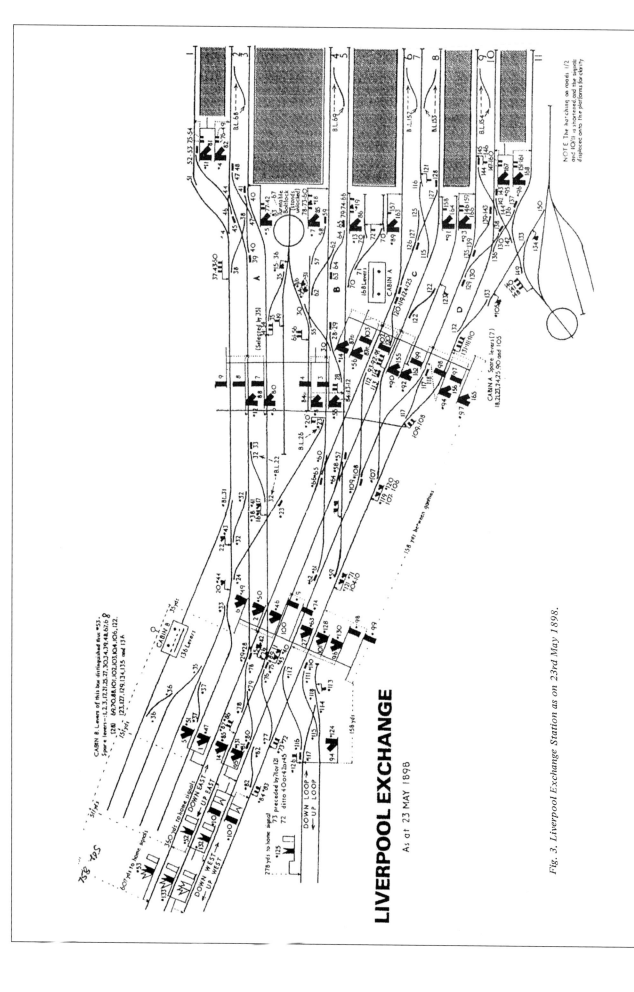

LIVERPOOL EXCHANGE

As at 23 MAY 1898

Fig. 3. Liverpool Exchange Station as on 23rd May 1898.

Plate 6. *Railways in their heyday! This picture portrays the Howard Street Goods Station c.1912/3. The viaduct leading to Exchange Station crosses the centre of the picture with the elevated Exchange 'B' Box on the right. The L&Y Railway sequentially numbered their signal boxes, with 'B' box being No. 423. It was built by the Railway Signal Company in 1886 and contained 136 levers. Exchange 'B' box was renamed No. 1 box when the resignalling took place. In the far distance, beyond the warehouse, the ex-LNWR Waterloo Dock branch passed beneath the ex-L&Y lines.*
L & Y SOCIETY

larger station at street level. The year 1886 saw the last use of Tithebarn Street Station, by which time there were 216 trains daily, arrivals and departures. The old station was often referred to as 'Exchange' being next to the well-known Cotton Exchange.

The new Exchange station was signalled by the Railway Signal Company in 1886 and four platform faces (platforms 1–5) were in use from 12th December, including the new four-track approach. Enlargement continued on both sides and on 2nd July 1888 the new station with ten platform faces was completed and opened. The Midland ran a through service to Scotland from the opening. Exchange Hotel was opened on 8th August in the same year. The electric train service to Southport was inaugurated on 22nd March 1904 (the line to Ormskirk was also electrified with full service from 1st May, 1913). The situation

then remained unchanged apart from severe bomb damage in 1940, with repairs only fully completed in 1954.

On Saturday 3rd August 1968 Exchange Station had the honour of receiving the very last scheduled British Railways steam-hauled standard-gauge passenger train from Preston; the locomotive was ex-LMS 'Black 5' 45318, the train being the Liverpool portion of a Glasgow to Liverpool and Manchester train. Main-line services ceased on 3rd May 1970, following which the station became just a suburban terminal, eventually closing on 29th April 1977, although the Exchange Booking Office remained open until Sunday 1st May for tickets for rail-replacement bus services.

Following closure, Southport trains were routed into Moorfields underground station which opened on Monday 2nd May 1977 by a connecting tunnel built some

200 yards back up the line using the west side of the old Great Howard Street Yard and the site of platforms 8 to 10 that allowed through running to Garston – the 'Link Line' of Merseyrail. Exchange platforms and roof were demolished to become a car park for offices in the old Exchange building that was retained and is now preserved. The original station clock is still in place and is wound by hand daily.

THE SCHEME
This scheme seems to have come about as a result of proposals for signal renewals by the S&T Dept rather than a grand plan by the Operating Dept. At the Works Committee meeting held on 27th October 1937 (minute 4537), a sum of £2591 was approved for the provision of new semaphore signal gantries in place of semaphore signal posts attached to the parapet walls of

Liverpool Exchange viaduct. The sighting forms for these gantries may have been in the S.S.15xx series but very few pre-war ones have survived. Perhaps it should be explained that signals were 'sighted' by a small committee who met on site to agree the position of a signal, ensuring the driver had the best view possible of the signal the train was approaching. Possibly under a separate authority, and maybe as a result of the routine renewal programme, S&T Dept (Western Division) plan 39–187 was drawn up that also included some of the platform starting signals, which were sighted for replacement as colour-light signals on 5th August 1942 (S.S. 5696 & 5697). This would seem to be under the authority of HQ Order 7801/6046. 'B' Box down starting and up home signals, on the same 4-line gantry, were sighted for colour-light signals on a new gantry on 4th June that year (S.S. 5763). After the formation of the New Works section, they became involved in the scheme and a new plan, NW43001, was issued including all these renewals and possibly also others. A further Western Division plan 44–72H for Exchange Station Junction may have been the wiring for the proposed re-signalling.

A gantry for 'Exchange' (possibly Manchester) was ordered from the RSC on 1st July 1941 (S.O. 1043) and four gantries for Liverpool Exchange Junction on 24th December the same year (S.O. 1391), and may actually have been delivered, but the work authorised in 1937 was never carried out, leading to the cancellation of the work at the Works Committee meeting on 20th November 1945 (minute 33). Authority was then presumably sought to provide colour light signals in their place together with comprehensive colour light signalling at Exchange Station 'A' and 'B' Signal Boxes and certain signals at Exchange Station Junction Signal box at a cost of £31,425. The sighting forms for the remainder of the signals in the scheme do not seem to have survived.

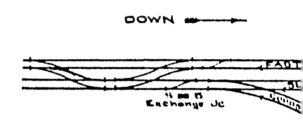

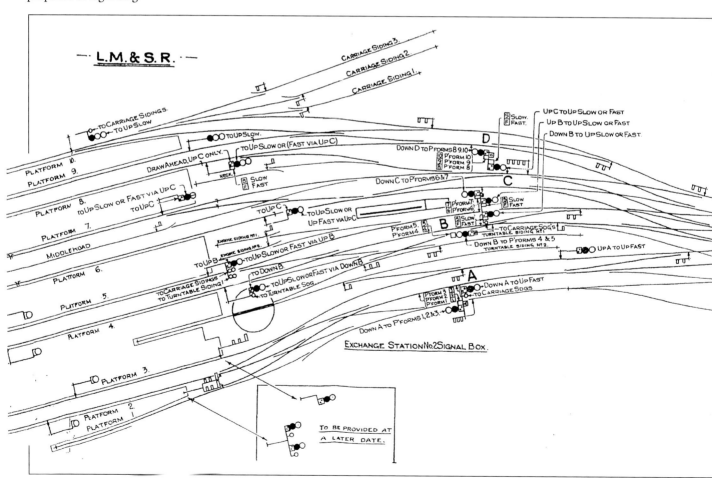

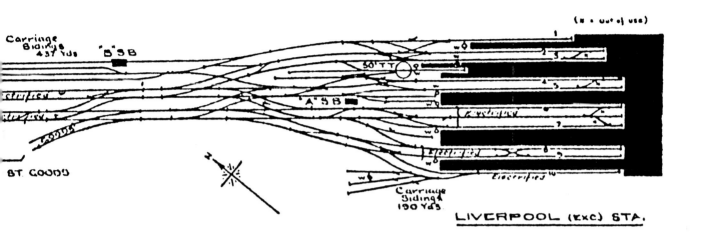

Fig. 2. An extract from the LMS Strip Diagram c.1935.

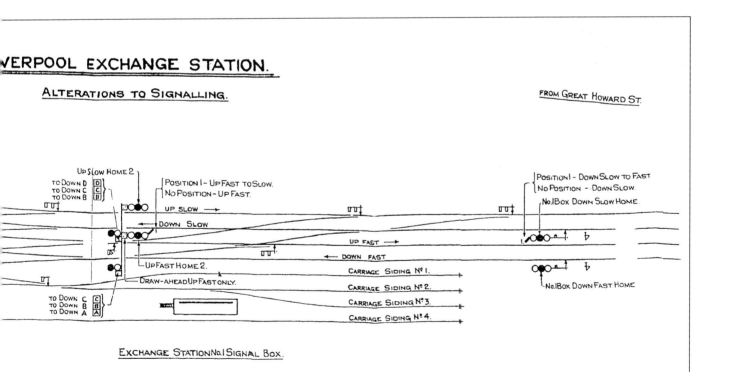

Figs. 4A & 4B. The main part of plan included with the Special Notice bringing the scheme into use on 26th May 1946.

Plate 4. *Liverpool Exchange No. 1 box (originally 'A') taken in 1949. The box opened with a temporary layout on 2nd December 1886 (with only four plat forms) and with the final layout on 12th December 1886. The box was of Railway Signal Company design with a 136-lever RSC frame, listed as 128 working and 8 spares. Due to structural deterioration the box was closed in 1962 and, after the removal of the frame, the box started to collapse. The structure was apparently pulled down complete into the street behind the box using steel cables.*

E. M. JOHNSON

SIGNAL BOXES AND STATION

Three signal boxes were involved – Exchange 'A', Exchange 'B' and Exchange Station Junction, all three actually dating from the 1886 Railway Signal Company scheme. Exchange Station Junction controlled the divergence for the branch to Great Howard Street Goods station where there was a smaller box dating from 1898 with 30 levers. Exchange Station Junction was destroyed and Great Howard Street Box damaged in the blitz of 21st-22nd Dec 1940 (see *LMS Journal No. 18* page 43). Both boxes were replaced by standard LMS boxes with 60 and 10 levers respectively. The new Junction box was in the 'V' of the goods branch divergence, 170 yards nearer the terminus than the old one. Track circuits 10313 to 10321 were brought into use on 29th February 1941, which date may also be the commissioning date of the replacement box. The new Great Howard Street box was only a signal but worked as a ground frame with no block working from the Junction SB.

The section between Exchange Station Junction and Sandhills No. 1 Box was almost a mile that was split by an Intermediate Block Section on all four lines at Milford Street with semaphore arms on a gantry. The IBS on the Down and Up Slow were installed in 1907 to facilitate the running of the improved electric service.

Those on the Fast lines were installed by the LMS. The Down Fast signal was installed on 2nd April 1939 (TCs 9391 & 9392) and the one on the Up Fast about the same time.

'B' box was badly damaged by fire in a raid in April or May 1941 (most likely 4th May 1941), as stated in *LMS Journal 18*. The Exchange signal boxes were renamed in the scheme, 'A' box becoming No. 2 and 'B' box No. 1. The boxes retained their lever frames as no power frame was included in this scheme. Exchange platforms were originally referred to as roads but well before the re-signalling scheme were renamed platforms. Prior to 1937, Roads 1 to 11 became Platforms 1 to 10, except for road 7 between new platform lines 6 and 7 that became 'Middle Siding'. For operational purposes, the station was divided into four areas: Groups A, B, C and D comprising platforms 1 to 3, 4 and 5, 6 and 7, 8 to 10 respectively. The Fast and Slow lines approaching from Sandhills split at No. 1 box (136 levers) into four pairs of lines each serving one Group of platforms. Group D was accessible from the Slow lines only. No. 2 box, with 168 levers, controlled the crossovers and sidings at the platform ends; it was only 237 yards from No. 1. The Slow lines and the lines serving platforms 6 to 10 were electrified.

In 1962, the elevated Exchange No. 1 Signal Box was replaced by a BR London Midland Region Type 15 box erected on the disused formation on the opposite (or up) side of the line. Thereafter reduction of facilities was effected in one scheme after another. Great Howard Street goods station was closed on 30th September 1963 but continued to be used for traffic to the sub-station and also van storage until 1964. Following this, S&T plan CS 420/64 detailed the removal of signalling and signalbox at Exchange Station Junction, which was not carried out at that time. Plans were changed, as frequently happened at that time. A further scheme for reduction of facilities between Bootle and Exchange was issued in 1967. Sandhills No. 1 SB (itself a large LMS installation with 145 levers dating from 1936) was abolished on 9th September 1968, and from then the Wigan line and the Southport line were separate routes as far as Exchange Station Junction. Abolition of Exchange Station Junction was finally carried out on 27th July 1969, so that the physical junction between the two routes was now at Exchange No. 1 box. During 1966 Exchange Junction was permanently switched out until 18th August 1968 when it was switched in again to facilitate the re-arrangement of the layout when all remaining points were disconnected. The box was switched in again

2.9.46.

LMS SIGHTING FORM FOR
INSTALLATION AND RENEWAL OF SIGNALS.

E.R.O. 50044

Serial No. XXXXX 5697
Div. Order No.
In Use

Memorandum of Meeting of Sighting Committee held at ___ LIVERPOOL EXCHANGE "A" BOX.'

Name and Lever No. of Signal(s) ___ Nos.1 & 2 platforms starting signals Nos.81 82.

Renewal Programme 19XX   Authority H.Q. Order 780/6X0X6   Ref'ce

Plan No. 39-187/3   Work

Division : Traffic CENTRAL   Sig. & Tel. WESTERN   Area WARRINGTON.

For Distant Signals only		PROPOSED.
Gradient-Level : Rising/Falling 1 in		Yds. Present ___ Proposed ___ From Home Signal
Max. : M.P.H. Allowable ___ Actual		Sighting Distance ___ Yards.
Classification of Line Most Important / Important / Unimportant		Control Indicator or and Underbolt exists/required in

EXISTING.

No Repeaters.

Slotted

82   81
76   75
49   54

23'-3"

R   L

10'-6"

Nº 2 Platform Line   Nº 1 Platform Line

PROPOSED.

Amendment referred to in memorandum. Plan No NW. 48001 other particulars as shown.

Water column 14" where oil

DRAWING REQUIRED

Minimum to clear structure gauge.

10'4"

Nº 2   P.1

To be fixed as far forward as Gauge Limits will allow.

Yds. from Box— Present 104   Proposed (103)

Is New Signal Required? YES

Type COLOUR LIGHT MULTI UNIT.

Method of Operation—Mech/XXXX

Power Available on site   Side of Line ___ Yds.

From

Is difficulty anticipated in Guying? No.   If so, state conditions

Centre of Post to Rails 5 Ft. 2 Ins.
Space between Rails 10 Ft. 4 Ins.
G.L. at Site 1 Ft. ___ Ins. XXXX/below R.L.
Standard depth in Ground (6 ft.) to be increased/decreased by ___ Ft.
Due to
Direction of Wire Pull— XXXXXXX Side

Remarks No.81 No.1 platform starting.   No.82 No.2 platform starting.
No.75 " " Shunt signal.   No.76 " " shunt signal.
No.54 " " to sidings.   No.49 " " to sidings.

(For continuance of Remarks see over)

We, the undersigned, jointly consider a Signal as proposed will be entirely satisfactory from our respective Departmental interests —

Committee T.E.Scott.
Controller J.V.Banks.   Motive Power Section C Watson.
Inspector J.Lewis.   Date 5th August, 1942.
Approved for T.W. Royle   Initialled by amendment   for A.F.Bound
Chief Operating Manager   Signal and Telegraph Engineer

Fig. 6A. In order to compensate for the lack of signal pictures, two examples of LMS Signal Sighting forms have been used. The sighting committee was made up of representatives of the Signal, Operating and Motive Power Departments who met on site to agree the arrangements for a new signal to ensure all parties were in accord with the proposals. The forms, Figs. 6A and 6B, refer to the two signals shown in the bottom centre of Fig. 4A shown as 'To be provided at a later date'. This form refers to the Platform 1 and 2 signals.

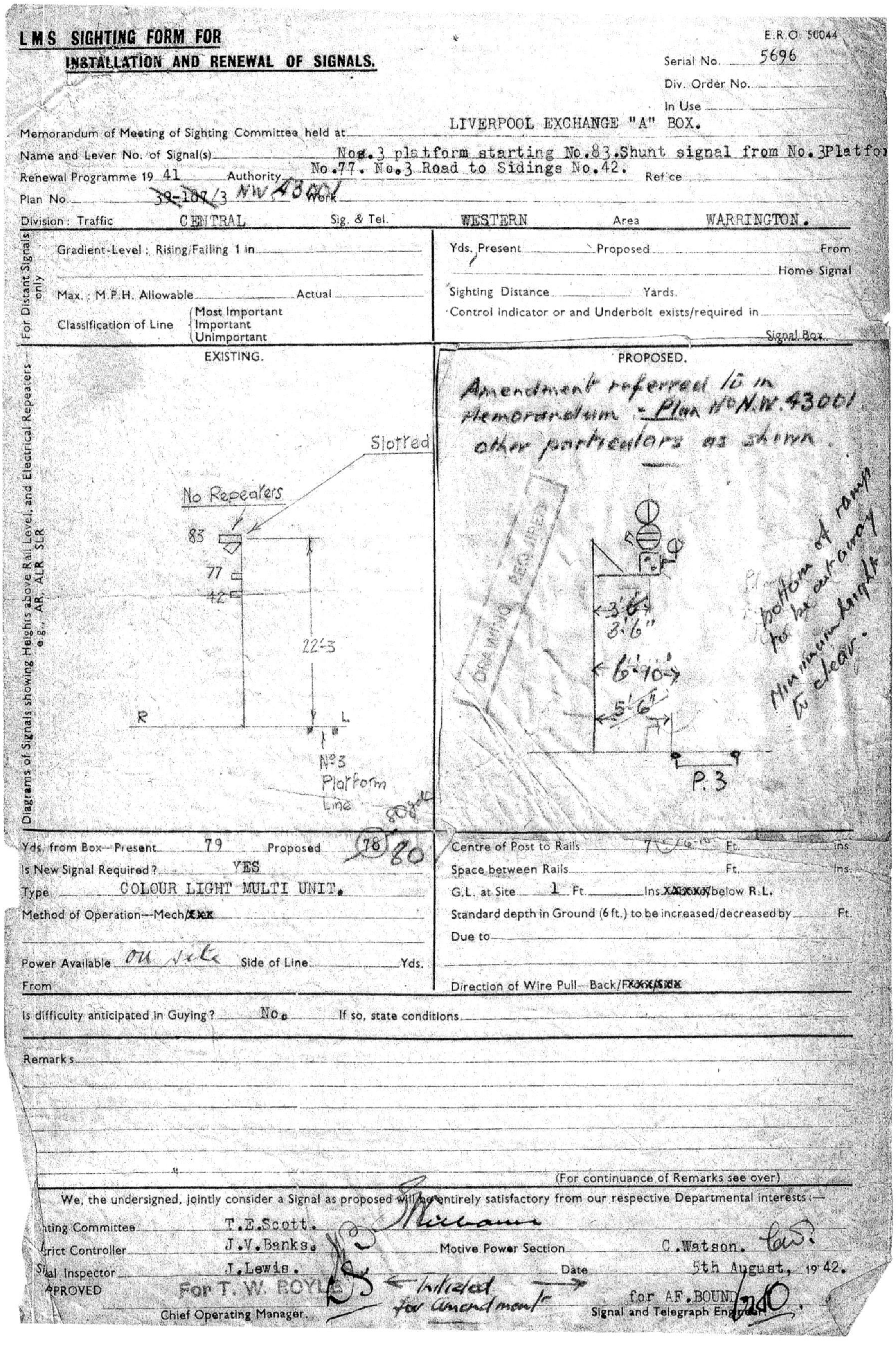

L M S SIGHTING FORM FOR

INSTALLATION AND RENEWAL OF SIGNALS.

E.R.O. 50044

Serial No. _5696_

Div. Order No. _____

In Use _____

Memorandum of Meeting of Sighting Committee held at _____ LIVERPOOL EXCHANGE "A" BOX.

Name and Lever No. of Signal(s) _____ Nos. 3 platform starting No.83. Shunt signal from No. 3 Platfor No.77. No. 3 Road to Sidings No. 42.

Renewal Programme 19 41 Authority _____ Ref'ce _____

Plan No. _____ 39-109/3 NW 43001 Work _____

Division : Traffic **CENTRAL** Sig. & Tel. **WESTERN** Area **WARRINGTON.**

For Distant Signals only —

Gradient-Level : Rising/Falling 1 in _____

Max. : M.P.H. Allowable _____ Actual _____

Classification of Line — Most Important / Important / Unimportant

Yds. Present _____ Proposed _____ From _____ Home Signal

Sighting Distance _____ Yards.

Control indicator or and Underbolt exists/required in _____ Signal Box.

Diagrams of Signals showing Heights above Rail Level, and Electrical Repeaters. e.g., AR, ALR, SLR

EXISTING.

Slotted

No Repeaters

83

77

42

22'-3

R   L

Nº 3
Platform
Line

PROPOSED.

Amendment referred to in memorandum — Plan Nº N.W. 43001 other particulars as shown.

3'6"
8'6"
6'90"
5'6"

P.3

bottom of ramp to be cut away minimum height to clear.

Yds. from Box—Present _79_ Proposed _78_ _80_

Is New Signal Required? _YES_

Type **COLOUR LIGHT MULTI UNIT.**

Method of Operation—Mech/Elec

Power Available _on site_ Side of Line _____ Yds.

From _____

Is difficulty anticipated in Guying? _No._ If so, state conditions _____

Centre of Post to Rails _7 6_ Ft. _____ Ins.

Space between Rails _____ Ft. _____ Ins.

G.L. at Site _1_ Ft. _____ Ins. above/below R.L.

Standard depth in Ground (6 ft.) to be increased/decreased by _____ Ft.

Due to _____

Direction of Wire Pull—Back/Front _____

Remarks _____

(For continuance of Remarks see over)

We, the undersigned, jointly consider a Signal as proposed will be entirely satisfactory from our respective Departmental interests :—

Sighting Committee _____ T.E.Scott.

District Controller _____ J.V.Banks.   Motive Power Section _____ C.Watson.

Signal Inspector _____ J.Lewis.   Date _____ 5th August, 1942.

APPROVED _____ For T. W. ROYLE   *Initialed for Amendment* →   for AF.BOUND

Chief Operating Manager.   Signal and Telegraph Engineer.

Fig. 6B. Sighting form for the Platform 3 signal.

permanently for signals only on 9th September 1968 to break the block section following the closure of Sandhills No. 1 box. On the 6th July 1969 the fast line signals were disconnected, thus signalling Slow line trains only with a new Intermediate Block Section (IBS) worked from Sandhills No. 2. On 27th July 1969 the box, together with Bank Hall box, closed with new IBS signals installed, worked from Exchange No. 1 box, Up Slow, and Bootle Junction Down Slow.

The line was reduced to two tracks between Sandhills and Exchange Station on 18th December 1973, by which time only platforms 4 to 7 remained in use. By this time the station was a shadow of its former status, with only a local train service. Platforms 1, 2 and 3 ('A' group) closed on 5th March 1967, with platforms 8, 9 and 10 ('D' group) closing on 6th May 1973, the latter to allow the construction of the new link line down to Moorfields. The remaining boxes were closed in 1977 together with Exchange Station. In July 1976 there were

still 301 trains every 24 hours. *Figure 7* details the alterations to the approach trackwork etc made between 1957 and 1964. It will be noted the designation of lines was reversed; Up became Down and vice versa after Exchange closed and the line ran down to Moorfields.

SIGNALS

The existing colour light signal from Platform line 6 was renewed 20 yards nearer No. 2 box. The colour light signal reading from Platform 7 was fixed 17 yards further from the box than the semaphore signal had been. Up advance signals at No. 2 box, slotted from No. 1 box, reading from roads 9, 10, 11 (renamed platform lines 8, 9, 10) were abolished and the controls from No. 1 box were taken back to the signals reading from platform lines 8, 9, 10.

Other than these modifications, all the new colour light signals that superseded semaphore signals were positioned at approximately the same distances and controlled by the same boxes as before. Two,

three and four-aspect signals were all utilised. As stated, the up and down lines leading to and from platforms 1, 2 and 3 were designated Up and Down Route A. The up and down lines leading to and from platforms 4 and 5 were designated Up and Down Route B. The up and down lines leading to and from platforms 6 and 7 were designated Up and Down Route C and the up and down lines leading to and from platform lines 8, 9 and 10 were designated Up and Down Route D.

Certain signals could be placed at danger before the whole train had passed :

No. 2 Box – From Down Route D to platforms 8, 9 and 10.
From Down Route C to platforms 6 and 7.
Exchange Station Junction Box – Down fast to slow home signals.

SIGNAL ASPECTS AND ROUTE INDICATORS
Position light junction indicators (feathers) were provided as for the Rugby scheme.

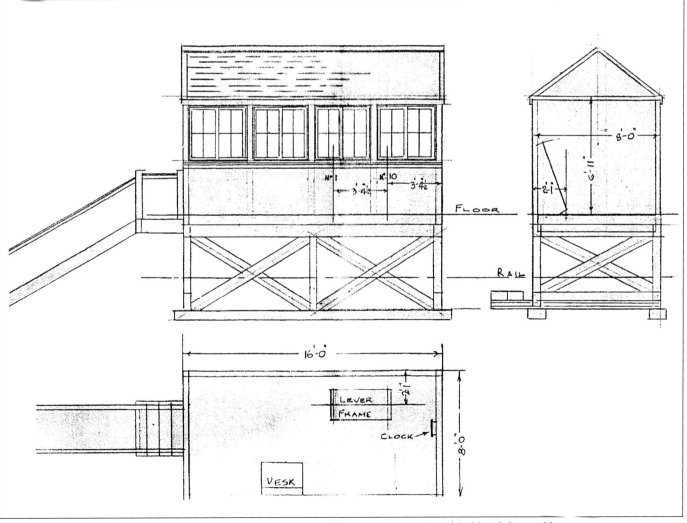

Fig. 8. The Great Howard Street 10-lever ground frame that replaced the original bomb-damaged box.

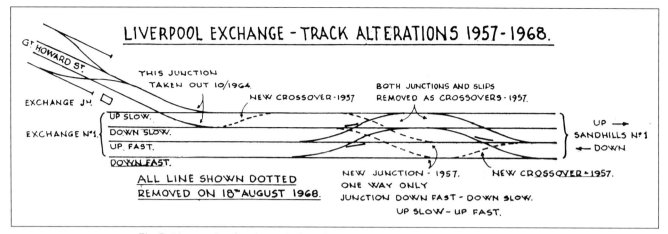

Fig. 7. Diagram showing the track alterations that took place between 1957 and 1969.

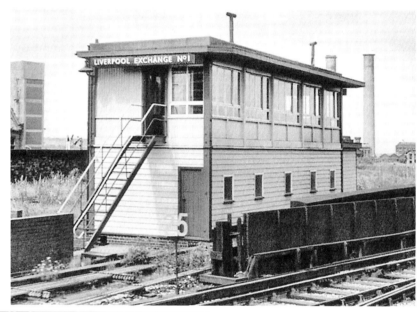

Plate 5. *Liverpool Exchange No. 1 box in July 1976 was an LMR type 15 box containing an LMR standard 85-lever frame that replaced the old elevated Railway Signal Company Exchange No. 1 box in 1962. This in turn was last used on 29th April 1977 but manned until 1st May for the dismantling of equipment. The box was built on the portion of viaduct that had formerly carried the connection between the Great Howard Street goods lines and the Slow lines at the station end, but which had been removed before 1946 (compare Figs. 2, 3 and 4B).* JAMES PAYNE

Plate 8. *Liverpool No. 1 box 85-lever frame taken in July 1976. Parts of the frame were later re-used at Ravenhead Junction in 1978.* TONY GRAHAM

Plate 10. *Looking from No. 2 box towards No. 1 in July 1976, showing all that was left of the sidings, with No. 1 box in the distance. The signals on the left are No. 2's starters coming off 'B' group.*
TONY GRAHAM

Plate 3. *Liverpool Exchange 'A' box as renamed No. 2, taken in 1970 from a train leaving Platform 7. The Railway Signal Company (RSC) box opened with a temporary layout on 2nd December 1886 (having only four platforms at that time) and fully opened on 12th December 1886. The box had a 168-lever RSC frame, many levers of which were replaced in 1965. Note the windows in the north gable end as the box tapered at that end due to the track formation. The front windows are of non-standard design, presumably due to being replaced following war bomb damage. The box was last used on 29th April 1977 but remained manned until 1st May 1977 for S&T work.*
JAMES PAYNE

Plate 7. *Liverpool Exchange No. 2 on 2nd July 1976, looking towards the No. 1 lever end. The LYR block instrument is still in use, unusually used in conjunction with a non-standard train describer specially manufactured in 1973 for the Exchange area. There were also two other pieces of non-standard equipment for signalling to No. 1 box introduced in 1973, being a 'B' or 'C' group indicator for incoming trains and a platform departure number indicator for outgoing trains. By this time there were only 48 working levers with 106 spare and 14 spaces.* TONY GRAHAM

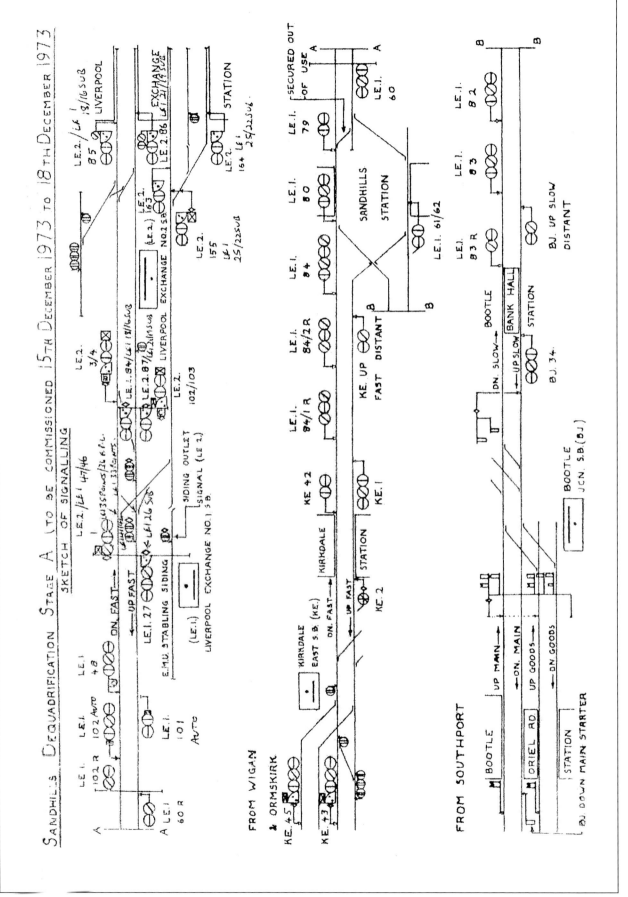

Fig. 5A. Liverpool Exchange in December 1973 when the trackwork was reduced from four to two lines approaching the station.

TONY GRAHAM

Theatre-type route indicators were used for indications to the routes A, B, C and D and platforms. Miniature green aspects were used for the diverging routes onto the Great Howard Street goods lines, which were worked under 'no Block' regulations and could be occupied, and those into the carriage sidings. Elevated position lights were also provided for subsidiary aspects on some signals including those reading into occupied platforms.

GROUND SIGNALS AND POINTS
The existing semaphore ground signals were retained and operated mechanically from the signal boxes as were the points.

POWER SUPPLY
This was obtained from the public supply authority, with a standby generating set provided that had originally been installed in an LMS ARP Control Shelter (Works Committee minute 404 of 28th November 1945).

SPECIAL NOTICE – (ERO 47910/5)
The scheme was brought into use at 12.01 a.m. on Sunday 26th May, 1946 although a couple of signals for platforms 1, 2 and 3 remained as semaphores and were to be replaced later (the relevant sighting forms have '6.9.46' pencilled on the top) and some colour light signals were already in use having replaced signals damaged in the blitz, colour lights being used in order to save fog-men:

No. 1 Box Up slow and Up Fast Starting.
Exchange Station Junction Down Slow and Down Fast Starting.
Exchange Station Junction Down Slow and Down Fast Home with route indicators.
See *Figures 4 & 4B.*

Acknowledgments
Public Record Office, Kew, Signalling Record Society Archive, Eddie Johnson and Trevor Moseley.

MULTI-ASPECT SIGNALS

3 ASPECT — G PROCEED / Y CAUTION BE PREPARED TO FIND NEXT SIGNAL AT STOP / R STOP

4 ASPECT — G PROCEED / Y Y WARNING BE PREPARED TO FIND NEXT SIGNAL AT CAUTION. / Y CAUTION BE PREPARED TO FIND NEXT SIGNAL AT STOP. / R STOP

Fig. 5B. Key to colour light aspects shown on Fig. 5A as extracted from IRSE booklet No. 1.

Plate 11. *Looking from No. 1 box towards Sand-hills, with all four lines still in use in 1973. The large works on the right is the Tate and Lyle sugar factory. Beneath the arches were a number of disused wagon turntables. The LNWR Waterloo goods cutting now partly infilled can be seen lower left.*
TONY GRAHAM

A Review of Wagon Books

by BOB ESSERY

The arrival of the latest wagon book, *LNWR Wagons Volume 2*, earlier this year prompted some 'editorial thoughts' that I would like to share with readers. On many local trip workings, a lot of time was spent in the Shunters Cabin where, between spells of work, the men were playing cards or dominoes, reading the newspaper or talking about sport, in particular horse racing. I found a better way of spending my time; I went wagon spotting. At this time my first crude attempt at building a model railway was underway and my prime interest was goods wagons. The year was 1953, and I recall spending some time wandering about the sidings looking at the various plates on wagon solebars. To my surprise, dates between 1900 and 1914 were not uncommon, whilst I even found some that were registered pre 1900. They were wooden-bodied ex-private owner wagons that were rapidly being replaced by 16-ton steel mineral wagons. Later I began to study the subject of wagons more carefully, and the first examples of my work appeared in the *Railway Modeller* during 1963.

Although *LMS Journal* and *Midland Record* are not modelling magazines, I try to publish information that will help produce accurate models. Whilst the preserved railways provide the feel of the steam railway, the mix of locomotives and rolling stock is not truly representative of the country branch line passenger services and certainly not as far as freight traffic was concerned. Looking back, I could see a link between this latest book and my early efforts that appeared in *Railway Modeller*. For me it all began when I received a letter from the late Cyril Freezer, asking me if I was interested in writing a book about British Goods Wagons; he had been asked by David & Charles if he could recommend an author. My answer was yes but I was not qualified to cover the subject, but I knew two men who could. The result was *British Goods Wagons* and whilst our names were in alphabetical order, Essery, Rowland and Steel, I was the junior partner. Published in 1970, it was to be the first of the modern wagon books and led to many others being published, including some under my name.

Looking at the array of titles on my bookshelf, it would appear that the LMS group is well covered but the big omission is the Scottish constituents of the LMS

company. However, a modeller does need to know what all the British railways companies built if he is to get a balanced mix of stock. It is also, all too easy to be left with the impression that the stock found on the railways was of relatively modern construction whereas pregroup rolling stock remained in service on British Railways well into the 1950s.

Turning now to *LNWR Wagons Volume 2*, I can clearly recall the start of the research that saw the first volume published in 2001. During the 1980s, my wife and I lived in Knowle and a close neighbour was David Clark who invited me to help him with a project designed to record the history of LNWR wagons. Whilst I was interested in the project, I felt that my workload would prevent me from playing a proper role, so I declined but offered him the use of my collection of wagon drawings and photographs. It is not Wild Swan policy to review its own books, so apart from the details given below I will now await Volume 3, and hope it will be less than ten years before it appears.

LNWR Wagons Volume 2

by The London & North Western Railway Society
Edited by Chris Northedge
Authors: Peter Ellis, Peter Davis, Dr Niall Ferguson
It has been a long time coming but the wait has been worthwhile. 220 pages, lots of pictures and drawings, softback at £29.95.

Starting with a detailed coverage of covered vans, this volume continues with vans for perishable traffic and miscellaneous vans including those for beer and gunpowder. Then we have a wide variety of trolleys of all shapes and sizes and conclude with appendices, etc. My personal opinion is that it is very good and a useful addition to any library of railway books.

OTHER WAGON BOOKS BY WILD SWAN

An Illustrated History of
LNER WAGONS Vol. 1 – Southern Area:
ex-Great Northern, ex-Great Central and ex-Great Eastern wagons absorbed by the LNER
by Peter Tatlow
256 pages. Casebound.
ISBN 1 905184 03 4. £34.95

LNER WAGONS Vol. 2 – North Eastern Area:
ex-H&B, ex-NE and ex-M&GN Wagons absorbed by the LNER
208 pages. Casebound.
ISBN 978 1 905184 34 7. £33.95

LNER WAGONS Vol. 3 – Scottish Area:
ex-North British and ex-Great North of Scotland wagons absorbed by the LNER
192 pages. Casebound.
ISBN 978 1 905184 56 9.
Vol. 4 in preparation

Midland Record Supplement No. 2
MIDLAND RAILWAY WAGONS
by R. J. Essery
48 pages. Laminated card cover.
ISBN 1 874103 45 3. £6.95

LNWR WAGONS Vol. 1
by the LNWR Society
216 pages. Casebound.
ISBN 1 874103 65 8. £26.95

LANCASHIRE & YORKSHIRE WAGONS Vol. 1
by Noel Coates
200 pages. Casebound.
ISBN 0 906867 87 8. £21.95

Vol. 2
264 pages. Casebound.
ISBN 1 905184 18 2. £35.95

NORTH STAFFORDSHIRE WAGONS
by G. F. Chadwick
96 pages. Laminated card cover.
ISBN 1 874193 15 1. £11.95

OFFICIAL DRAWINGS OF LMS WAGONS
by R. J. Essery
Vol. 1 – *out of print*

Vol. 2
72 pages. Laminated card cover.
ISBN 1 874103 33 X. £8.95

THE 4MM COAL WAGON
A Step-by-Step Guide
by John Hayes
160 pages. Laminated card cover.
ISBN 1 874103 48 8. £14.95

THE 4MM WAGON Part 1 – Opens, Minerals & Hoppers
by Geoff Kent
88 pages. Laminated card cover.
ISBN 1 874103 03 8. £12.95

Part 2 – General Merchandise Vans, Special Purpose Vans and Tank Wagons
160 pages. Laminated card cover.
ISBN 1 874103 24 0. £14.95

Part 3 – Conflats & containers, wagons for long loads & steel, brake vans and finishing touches
160 pages. Card cover.
ISBN 1 874103 97 6. £16.95

LMS TIMES

LMS JOURNAL No. 30

I have just started to subscribe to your *LMS Journal* at the age of 83. I have been a railway enthusiast for over 70 years, mostly LMS as I was brought up in my home town of Warrington.

Re the article 'LMS Parcels Traffic', I was intrigued by the photo on page 45 as I think it was taken at Warrington Bank Quay Station and not at St. Helens as captioned. Surely the shot shows Crosfields (Levers) Soap Works on the left and we are looking north. This is not a criticism as I may be mistaken. However, if it is Warrington BQ, I spent many hours on this station.

Incidentally, I had the privilege of being invited onto the footplate of 25350 *Coronation* before the new Coronation appeared. Would it be 1937 as she still carried her nameplates at the time? I can remember that it gave the build date and the information that it was the 5000th engine built at Crewe.

Bob Lee
Crewe

Mr. Lee is quite correct. [Editor]

The photo on page 15 of Birmingham New Street raises many questions in my mind. The train appears to be composed of LNWR stock built in 1911, and is an 11-coach set of 6-wheeled elliptical-roof coaches which were designated Birmingham and Sutton Coldfield sets. The engine head lamp indicates light engine, so was the engine about to run round the train? I was not aware that a Down train from Proof House Junction could proceed to Platform 1 from Birmingham New Street No. 1 SB. My recollection is Down trains were routed to either face of Platform 2 or to Platform 3. Is the photograph taken after a Down working from Sutton Coldfield to either Platforms 2 or 3, and then taken to the north tunnel and reversed into Platform 1 from Birmingham New Street No. 5 SB? The position of the locomotive is important, as any smoke would avoid a nuisance on the Stephenson Street footbridge.

My memory is that the south end pilot was always an LNWR coal tank, and the north end pilot an LNWR passenger or Watford tank.

Brian Hayes
by email

I consider myself fortunate in having lived beside and later worked for the LMS/LMR in the 30s, 40s and 50s. Although my railway interest had originally been caught by witnessing the inaugural run of the brand new 'Coronation Scot' in 1937 as it passed through Kings Langley, I soon began to appreciate the wide variety of pre-grouping motive power still in service. Many of the local trains, at that time, were hauled by LNW 'Prince of Wales' 4–6–0s and the goods trains still mostly headed by Super Ds. Visits to London found the approaches to Euston littered with Willesden-based 'Watford Tanks', 'Coal Tanks' and 'Cauliflowers' on empty stock workings. These did not leave the scene until 1946 when they were displaced by equally ancient Midland 2Fs that stayed in place until 1949.

By then I had been lucky enough to have served an Engineering Apprenticeship in Scotland where the ranks of former Caledonian engines had been largely left untouched — the first real withdrawals of the ubiquitous 'Jumbos' didn't begin until the late 1940s, for example, and the last remained at work until 1963. Stationed at St. Rollox, of course, I also saw the last of several outstanding classes, the 'Dunalastair' II and III 4–4–0s and 179 class 4–6–0s, for instance, not to mention the G&SW 2–6–0s and 0–6–2Ts.

When I turned up at Rowsley as Running Foreman in 1950 I found that it was not only a Midland shed, albeit opened in 1926, but that all but a handful of the engine allocation was of either Midland origin or design with not a few of the visiting freight engines being the sedulous Super Ds. All over the country, up to and beyond nationalization, branch line trains and freight trip workings were still being worked by pre-grouping engines. Take the Merthyr, Tredegar & Abergavenny and Cockermouth, Keswick & Penrith lines as cases in point — both were worked almost exclusively by LNW engines until the end of their days. So, I cannot but agree with the Editor that the LMS was far and away from being a Stanier railway.

Keith Miles
Seaton

The photo caption on page 72 refers to the Down Salop Independent Line at Crewe South Junction. In my period working at Crewe, from the mid-1960s and through the 1970s, I always understood that only the portion of line connecting Gresty Lane No. 1 and Salop Goods Junction SBs was referred to as the Salop Independent Lines, unless, of course, line designations had been changed between 1947 and 1966.

J. A. Smith
Shrewsbury

I am intrigued by the LMS consignment note for the carriage of milk (page 52) for it contrasts with my researches in other parts of the country. On the former GCR's London Extension, for example, former dairy farmers told me that the contract with the dairies covered the carriage charge in both directions. With one exception — if the milk on reaching the dairy was found to be 'off', it was sent back and the farmer obliged to pay the carriage; it was a neat part of the quality control.

Secondly, the volume of milk carried was quite flexible — it varied around the year, never mind from day to day from any particular farm for all sorts of reasons. The dairy contracts allowed the farmers to deliver all they could within reason and the amount received by the dairy would be measured (each churn contained a calibrated post), recorded, and the farmer paid accordingly. A practical consequence of these contracts is that during the spring, when the volume of milk peaked — unlike the winter months when it was at its lowest — the dairies could be embarrassed with a surplus.

Finally, milk delivery at the station was a fast and hectic procedure in which the motion of the staff checking the contents of each churn and the farmer having to fill in a form sounds completely impractical.

The only explanation I can offer for this form is that it was proposed and abandoned, or its sole application was for isolated carriage of milk outside the main flows.

One final point, the form refers to 'Imperial gallons'. In my encounters with dairy farmers, the standard unit was a 'barn gallon', which was 17 pints. Didn't we also have rods, roods and perches?

Steve Banks
Banbury

Unfortunately, an error crept in to the captioning of the drawing of signal boxes on page 22, which was missed by me and for which I sincerely apologise.

The original drawings which I hold in my possession were designed to assist the S&T Engineer's representative when attending a site meeting for a proposed new signal box. They were produced in a folder and showed all the sizings up to a No. 15. All the drawings were colour washed to show the external colour scheme of the proposed structure, but only the first sheet was used in the article together with the final two which showed the internal arrangements and the ordering pro-forma.

I have included the sizing information which may be of interest:

	Box size	Levers	Window sections
1	(17ft 10in x 11ft 4in)	10	2 x 8ft
2	(19ft 10in x 11ft 4in)	15	1 x 10ft and 1 x 8ft
3	(21ft 10in x 11ft 4in)	20	2 x 10ft
4	(26ft 4in x 13ft 10in)	25 & 30	3 x 8ft
5	(28ft 4in x 13ft 10in)	35	1 x 10ft and 2 x 8ft
6	(30ft 4in x 13ft 10in)	40 & 45	1 x 8ft and 2 x 10ft
7	(34ft 10in x 13ft 10in)	50 & 55	4 x 8ft
8	(38ft 10in x 13ft 10in)	60 & 65	2 x 8ft and 2 x 10ft
9	(43ft 4in x 13ft 10in)	70 & 75	5 x 8ft
10	(45ft 4in x 13ft 10in)	80 & 85	1 x 10ft and 4 x 8ft
11	(47ft 4in x 13ft 10in)	90	3 x 8ft and 2 x 10ft
12	(51ft 4in x 13ft 10in)	95 & 100	1 x 8ft and 4 x 10ft
13	(55ft 10in x 13ft 10in)	105 & 110	4 x 8ft and 2 x 10ft
14	(59ft 10in x 13ft 10in)	115 & 120	2 x 8ft and 4 x 10ft
15	(60ft 4in x 13ft 10in)	125	7 x 8ft

The window arrangements for the ends were 1 x 8ft and 1 x 4ft (steps end). The remaining width was made up with a timber panel or timber panel plus door.

Trevor Moseley
by email

An amendment to the caption accompanying Gordon Hepburn's superb photograph on pages 19/20: I'm afraid we're at Nottingham Midland station on the through roads between Platforms 3 and 4. No. 1327 is standing on a siding used for stock not immediately required with the 'Middle loop' next to it. The date is March 1933 and the carriages are those of a Mansfield service. In the background, above the third carriage, is Nottingham Passenger East box with London Road bridge dimly visible beyond that.

The picture on page 52 of No. 5535 *Sir Herbert Walker* quite puzzled me as I couldn't understand why a fully complete main-line train was sitting on the wrong line at Cricklewood. The train is indeed wrong line on the up fast. Several clues which didn't strike me immediately — the 20A code of Leeds Holbeck, the driver looking forward for signals and the head lamp code — milk train consisting of coaching stock or equivalent. The train has been worked across from the Express Dairies sidings, a quite complex move, and is now about to move forward and gain the down fast via a crossover just beyond the Acton lines, all controlled by Cricklewood Junction. Date? Perhaps late 30s. Holbeck had several Patriots until Stanier brought out his Jubilees which replaced the majority of them. I think we're looking at empties returning north, perhaps to Appleby Dairy, also owned by Express, on the Settle and Carlisle section. I've seen other pictures describing the workings as bound for Carlisle. All in all a fascinating picture that Dr. Ransome-Wallis captured for us.

J. Richard Morton
Beauchief, Sheffield

VARIOUS ISSUES

I've been meaning to write for some time re queries in *LMS Journal*. These are not intended to be comprehensive notes (because I don't have the time to do the research for sources), but here goes!

You have asked about the circumstances re the removal of side lamps from coaching stock. This was the result of the multiple accident at Alne near York, see *http://www.railwaysarchive.co.uk/ documents/MoT_Alne1933.pdf*

Re CLC motive power in a recent *LMSJ*, it was decided very early on in the history of the CLC that the MS&L would provide engines for internal CLC trains of all descriptions because the GNR didn't have loco servicing facilities in the area. Judging by the recent reply in *LMSJ*, this was later unsuccessfully challenged, but my researches haven't yet got beyond the 1860s.

You asked a long time ago for the meaning of the word 'freight'. My understanding is that this word dates from the time before the railways, when all transport was hauled by horses/mules on the roads. 'Freighting' is to do with a wagon carrying more than one item, but for different customers/destinations. The present road haulage business calls it, I understand, 'groupage'. The term seems to have lost favour in the UK quite early in our railway history, but in the US/Canada the term seems to have been adopted by railway/ railroad companies directly from the road haulage companies and became synonymous with all non-passenger workings. It was later imported (by the LMS?) and applied, again, for all non-passenger work excepting parcel/packet work, which is the classic application of the term 'freight'. Hope that helps.

David Mylchreest
by email

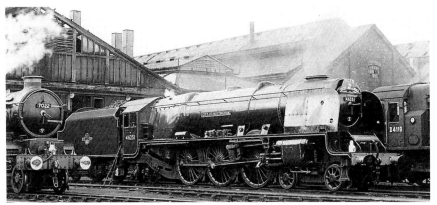

As you say you do not know the reason for 46251 being on shed at Annesley (cover photo LMSJ 24), I can confirm that it was there in connection with an RCTS Railtour 'The East Midlander' from Nottingham to Swindon on 9th May 1964. I also enclose two photos which may be of some interest — 46251 at Nottingham Victoria ready to depart to Swindon, and the same engine 'on shed' at Swindon.

B. T. Beers
Nottingham